The 2012 Political Contest in America
Conversations with a Gadfly

Ronald J. Scott, Jr.

DEDICATION

This book is dedicated to my father, who taught me to seek the truth.

CONTENTS

ACKNOWLEDGMENTS

Many family members, friends, and professional colleagues offered encouragement, feedback, and advice on a variety of sensitive topics in this book. Three professional colleagues examined statistical analyses presented. They support the robustness and rigor of the approach and the validity of the findings.

I thank Perini & Associates for their support, advice, and encouragement in extending the reach of ideas presented in this book. I look forward to a fruitful partnership with them.

In the interest of full disclosure, three close friends were offended by views expressed on topics in the book. I regret this. Someday I hope friends, and even complete strangers, will be more willing to entertain rationale for diversity in worldviews.

I especially thank my wife, Mary, for tolerating my passion to understand the dynamics of what is taking place in American politics.

Unless otherwise indicated (e.g., government graphics in the public domain), all graphics were developed by me. Data for statistical analysis presented in this book are from the U.S. federal government. The political power algorithm at Appendix B is my invention.

Permission to use the American Civil War cartoon on the cover of the book was granted by Bill Darcy of History Gallery (http://historygallery.com). Credits for photographs contained in the book follow:

p. 3, *The Iron Curtain*, Orange.man, Wikimedia Commons (Public Domain)

p.4, a collage of *The Coffee Cup Café, Serrano's Coffee, and O'Malley's Pub & Grill*, taken by Ronald J. Scott, Jr., and used with permission

p. 4, the *Gadfly Corner* image developed by the author. The rendition of Socrates was developed by John Paul MacIsaac for, and is the property of, Ronald J. Scott, Jr.; used with permission

p. 5, *René Descartes*, After Frans Hals, Wikimedia Commons (Public Domain)

p. 6, *Friedrich A. Hayek*, Dick Clark Mises, Wikimedia Commons (Public Domain)

p. 6, *Nicolaus Copernicus*, http://www.frombork.art.pl/Ang10.htm, Wikimedia Commons (Public Domain)

p. 7, *George Lakoff*, Flickr: Pop!Tech 2008 - George Lakoff, Wikimedia Commons (Public Domain)

p. 10, *President George W. Bush*, Eric Draper, Wikimedia Commons (Public Domain)

p. 14, *Senator Harry Reid*, http://reid.senate.gov/images/Reid-_2009_Official_Photo.jpg, Wikimedia Commons (Public Domain)

p. 14, *Congresswoman Nancy Pelosi*, (2013) *113th Congress, Congressional Pictorial Directory*, Government Printing Office, p. XIII, Wikimedia Commons (Public Domain)

p. 14, *Speaker John Boehner*, http://republicanleader.house.gov/Bio/, Wikimedia Commons (Public Domain)

p. 15, *Joseph Schumpeter*, http://commons.wikimedia.org/wiki/File:Mises,hayek,shumpe.jpg, Wikimedia Commons (Public Domain)

p. 20, *President Barack Obama*, Pete Souza, Wikimedia Commons (Public Domain)

p. 33, *President William Jefferson Clinton*, Bob McNeely, Wikimedia Commons (Public Domain)

p. 43, *President Ronald Reagan*, http://www.dodmedia.osd.mil/DVIC_View/Still_Details.cfm?SDAN= DASC9003096&JPGPath=/Assets/Still/1990/Army/DA-SC-90-03096.JPG, Wikimedia Commons (Public Domain)

p. 53, *Clint Eastwood*, gdcgraphics at http://flickr.com/photos/gdcgraphics/, Wikimedia Commons (Public Domain)

p. 55, *Secretary of State John Kerry*, State Department, Wikimedia Commons (Public Domain)

p. 61, *Fyodor Dostoevsky*, Konstiantyn Trutovsky, Wikimedia Commons (Public Domain)

p. 63, *President Abraham Lincoln*, Alexander Gardner, Wikimedia Commons (Public Domain)

p. 66, *Portrait of Baruch de Spinoza (1632-1677), ca. 1665,* author unknown, Wikimedia Commons (Public Domain)

p. 69, *David Axelrod*, Pete Souza, Wikimedia Commons (Public Domain)

p. 70, *President Woodrow Wilson*, Harris & Ewing, Wikimedia Commons (Public Domain)

p. 71, *Governor Mitt Romney*, Gage Skidmore, Wikimedia Commons (Public Domain)

p. 71, *Congressman Paul Ryan*, http://paulryan.house.gov/uploadedphotos/highresolution/3f3943d8-cea4-4f6b-96ac-3c25fd3ef24e.jpg, Wikimedia Commons (Public Domain)

p. 73, *Tea Party Protest*, Freedom Fan, Wikimedia Commons (Public Domain)

p. 73, *Nicholas Kristof*, World Economic Forum from Cologny, Switzerland, 30 January, 2012, Wikimedia Commons (Public Domain)

p. 73, *Thomas Friedman*, Charles Haynes, Wikimedia Commons (Public Domain)

p. 73, *Joe Nocera*, Doc Searls, Wikimedia Commons (Public Domain)

p. 73, *Maureen Dowd*, Maureen Dowd, Wikimedia Commons (Public Domain)

p. 75, *President John F. Kennedy*, Cecil Stoughton, Wikimedia Commons (Public Domain)

p. 77, *George Orwell*, Branch of the National Union of Journalists (BNUJ), Wikimedia Commons (Public Domain)

p. 78, *Vladimir I. Lenin*, Soyuzfoto, Wikimedia Commons (Public Domain)

p. 78, *Adolph Hitler*, Heinrich Hoffman, Wikimedia Commons (Public Domain)

p. 79, *Secretary of State Hillary Clinton*, Technical Sergeant Jacob N. Bailey, U.S. Air Force/Released, Wikimedia Commons (Public Domain)

p. 83, *Deputy Secretary of State Richard Armitage*, U.S. Government, Wikimedia Commons (Public Domain)

p. 83, *Secretary of State Colin Powell*, Charles Haynes, Wikimedia Commons (Public Domain)

p. 87, *President Thomas Jefferson*, Rembrandt Peale, Wikimedia Commons (Public Domain)

p. 89, *Aldous Huxley*, Khutuck at tr.wikipedia, Wikimedia Commons (Public Domain)

p. 103, *John Stuart Mill*, *Popular Science Monthly* Volume Three, Wikimedia Commons (Public Domain)

p. 139, *Ronald J. Scott, Jr.*, taken by the author, used with permission

1 INTRODUCTION

The purpose of this book is to sound an alarm about the progressive movement in America. The alarm is based on an accumulation of indisputable evidence. Three major events motivated me to sound the alarm.

The first event occurred during a visit to Washington, D.C. The year was 2006, and I had just completed a week's worth of research and analysis as a member of a high level team working on nuclear counterterrorism. While walking through the Reagan International Airport for a return flight to Monument, Colorado, I noticed numerous copies of a book prominently displayed at the Border's Book Store: *Whose Freedom: The Battle over America's Most Important Idea*, by George Lakoff.[1] I glanced through a copy while standing in the book store. There was no index, nor were there any citations, endnotes, or footnotes. The book jacket accused George W. Bush and the political right wing of "hijacking" the idea of freedom. Lakoff seemed to have an impressive academic pedigree--a cognitive scientist at the University of California at Berkeley. I bought the book. I read the book. And this was my first serious introduction to the modern progressive movement. I sought out and read all of Lakoff's works--books and journal articles--and learned how passionate Lakoff and others of his worldview are about this ideology, or orthodoxy, that is progressivism.

The second event, in March 2011, was a friendly conversation over coffee with a close friend, a retired senior officer from the military. Out of the blue, my friend announced he was a progressive. I asked what that

---

[1] George Lakoff, *Whose Freedom? The Battle over America's Most Important Idea*, (New York, NY: Farrar, Straus and Giroux, 2006).

1

meant, and he replied, "You know, I'm for progress: better education, better quality of life, and so forth." My response was "Who isn't? But, what does progressive mean from a political perspective?" He replied, "I do not know." Within months I began to discover many of my senior military colleagues were aligning themselves with the symbols (emotive language) and slogans (hope and change) of the Obama cohort. Ironically, these symbols and slogans were reminiscent of other disciples (e.g., Vladimir Lenin, Woodrow Wilson, Joseph Stalin, Franklin Roosevelt, Mao Tse Tung, Fidel Castro, Lyndon Johnson, Hugo Chavez, and now Barack Obama) of the Marxist progressive movement, without knowing (or recalling) the history or understanding the actual meaning of progressivism and its insidious momentum and impact within the American culture.

These two experiences then stirred a distant memory of another event. In 1979, my family and I moved to Sembach Air Base, West Germany for a three-year assignment as a forward air controller, flying the OV-10B. My family and I were aware of what the Cold War was all about. My mission involved being part of the coalition of forces that would blunt any Soviet and Warsaw Pact attempt to penetrate the Fulda Gap. Yet, all of this was relatively fictional to us until January 1980 when Mary and I traveled on a French troop train from Karlsruhe, West Germany to Berlin, East Germany. We had a private sleeping berth with a large window to the outside. We could not sleep. We drank French wine and ate French pâté and crackers while enjoying the passing scenery. I was reading *A Time for Truth* by William Simon.[2] Then, we crossed the border into East Germany. The train stopped about every 30 minutes. Each time, East German soldiers would form up along the entire length of the train on both sides. An East German officer boarded the train and examined all our documents.

Simon's book, which warned about the incremental advance of socialism in America, in combination with the visual images of East German totalitarianism made a huge impact on us. Simon provided an exceptional analysis to support his concerns. I reread the book after the discussion with my progressive friend. The corruption in *A Time for Truth* pales in comparison with what is currently going on in America.

The inspiration for the title of this book came from an 1862 essay by John Stuart Mill: "The Contest in America."[3] As Mill pointed out, contests that use human instruments in the service of a master degrade

---

[2] William E. Simon, *A Time for Truth*, (New York, NY: Berkley Publishing Corporation, 1978).

[3] John Stuart Mill, "The Contest in America," *Fraser's Magazine*, April 1862. This essay is in the public domain and available at
http://www.gutenberg.org/cache/epub/5123/pg5123.txt

them. The implications of not checking the current political direction in America is that while some elite may win the contest, millions will become degraded and miserable creatures. The cartoon on this book cover appeared three months after Mill's essay in the British *Punch Magazine*, and is used with permission from the copyright holder. It is a sober reminder of the costs associated with "sensational" political contests.

Figure 1. The Iron Curtain that Separated Eastern Europe from Western Europe

Most of the reflections and analysis in the chapters that follow are presented in the form of a conversation. Meet our conversationalists: IM (a fictitious American citizen with an inquiring mind) and Old Gadfly (me).

Chapter 2, "Cogito Ergo Sum," sets the stage, introduces the notion of a growing population of Copernican drones, and the importance of critical thinking. This chapter is a monologue by Old Gadfly. Chapter 3, "The 'Inherited Economy' Narrative," Chapter 4, "Taxes, Unemployment, and Public Debt," and Chapter 5, "The Art of Economy Surfing," present critical analysis on the economy and attempt to portray a more accurate picture regarding causal factors. It was unavoidable in such an analysis not to expose which parties should be responsible and accountable for issues related to the economy. Chapter 6, "An Empty Chair," and Chapter 7, "Dry, Parched Lips," are conversations about the Republican and Democratic National Conventions, respectively, and the implications of progressive ideology. Chapter 8, "Engineering Public Sentiment," and Chapter 9, "Memetics and Politics," analyze the evidence related to the disingenuous progressive political manipulation of public sentiment. Chapter 10, "Takers Are Pathetic Fools," Chapter 11, "Political Prostitution," and Chapter 12, "Honeymoon Tonight, Marriage Tomorrow?" address motivations of individual behaviors. Chapter 13 closes with two major conclusions and corresponding implications.

With the exception of the monologue in the second chapter that took place in the Washington D.C. area, the remaining chapters are conversations that took place in Monument and Palmer Lake, Colorado. Settings for the conversations were at The Coffee Cup Café and Serrano's Coffee in Monument and O'Malley's Pub & Grill in Palmer Lake. These are ordinary public settings where we were surrounded by ordinary people.

The chapters in this book have been vetted through my blog:

Gadfly Corner
Analysis and Reflections

You can visit the blog at http://gadflycorner.blogspot.com/. The material, with some adaptation, is used in this book with permission.

This book is the first of a series of books that analyze and reflect upon current affairs in America. The goal is to build a foundation for a capstone book on the art of peace. This book begins with who and where we are in America.

Ronald J. Scott, Jr.
Monument, Colorado

2 "COGITO ERGO SUM"

August 9, 2012
While wondering about in Washington, D.C.

René Descartes is known for his observation, "cogito ergo sum," which when translated from Latin to English means "I think therefore I am." This is a profound statement. It declares that human beings, with their innate capacity to think, can achieve awareness. Lesser forms behave in ways to adapt to their environments. One-cell amoebas behave in ways to survive. Dandelions in my yard physically orient toward the sun. Yet, neither of these two forms can achieve awareness.

What is the rationale for this book? The book presents reflective and analytical conversations between Old Gadfly and an American citizen with an inquiring mind, known as IM, about a world that is becoming increasingly complex, absurd, and ripe for catastrophic unintended consequences.

We inherited libraries and artifacts of great wisdom and methods for scientific inquiry. We enjoy the conveniences stemming from technology. Yet, we seem to be losing a collective capacity to reason--to think clearly, to discern the finer qualities of distinction among differences, to achieve awareness. Humans are equipped to do more than survive or to spontaneously orient toward pleasure or away from discomfort. Yet,

Americans have been trained or programmed, as in Pavlov's dog, to suppress this capacity for awareness.

In his 1944 book, *The Road to Serfdom*, Friedrich. A. Hayek warned against the pathologies of political correctness we currently witness and experience in his chapter, "The End of Truth." Hayek observed that in societies sliding toward, or completely overcome by, totalitarianism, it is not sufficient for citizens to **acknowledge** (i.e., to tolerate without affirmation or advocacy) values prescribed by the political elite; to the contrary, members of society are expected to spontaneously and emotionally react to anything that challenges or threatens those values--that is, spontaneously  orient toward the collective freedom enabled by prevailing political dogma and away from any challenge to that dogma.[4] Have you ever encountered a conversation when another person gets angry about something you said related to political values? It happens a lot nowadays.

Sadly, some readers may be incapable of comprehending the analysis and reflections in the conversations contained in this book. Most of these people are *Copernican drones*, and many are the product of a public school education system that spends more time prescribing what to think instead of how to think. These Copernican drones lack the functional capacity to pollinate the world with enduring ideas based on their own creative thinking or critical analysis.

Nicolaus Copernicus published only one book in his lifetime--*On the Revolutions of the Celestial Spheres*--and it sparked a scientific revolution. In the introduction to his book, there is a discussion about Copernicus's reluctance to officially publish his analysis and theory of the solar system. He knew that it would receive harsh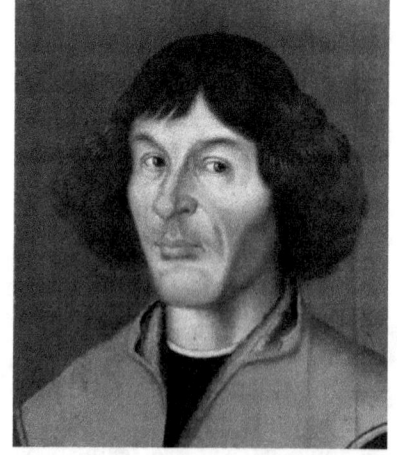

---

[4] F.A. Hayek, *The Road to Serfdom*, Text and Documents, The Definitive Edition, (London, UK: The University of Chicago Press, 2007 [1944]), p. 171.

criticism--not from the few who would take the time to digest his work first hand, but from the "drones among bees," who claimed to be experts but only repeated what other drones such as themselves have written in newspapers and magazines.[5] In other words, the drones repeated sound bites such as those we hear on the nightly news, or read in newspapers or magazines like the modern era's *Newsweek* that substitute trivia for the deeper analysis that can bring us more meaningful approximations of truth.

Even our academics seem to be losing a capacity for lucidity and depth of reasoning. Should not academia be the one sector in our society where knowledge is advanced through reasoning, that is, through the spatial reasoning, conscious thought, and language that takes place in the neocortex of our brains?

Yet, this potential "neocortex" function of academia is subordinate to a political orientation that derives from what Paul MacLean, in his book, *The Triune Brain in Evolution: Role in Paleocerebral Functions*, calls the "paleomammalian complex" portion of our brains.[6] It is this portion where the functions of long-term memory, emotion, and motivation take place. This portion of the human brain also is where political framing originates and resonates. Frankly, today's hubristic scholarship is devolving to mere flotsam, drifting on the surface of an immense ocean of potential knowledge.

To cite just one example, read the work of George Lakoff, whose publications represent mostly old wine in new bottles. The wine in Lakoff's case is a system of normative values. His "wine" prescribes a world the way he, and those who subscribe to the same politically correct values, thinks it should be. Lakoff even claims in his book *Thinking Points: Communicating Our American Values and Vision* that it is the frame that matters--if facts fit, great; if not, then the facts do not matter.[7] Scholars such as Lakoff do **not** seek to

---

[5] Nicolaus Copernicus, *On the Revolutions of the Heavenly Spheres*, in Robert. M. Hutchins (Ed.) Great Books of the Western Word, Volume 16, pp. 499-838, (Chicago, IL: Encyclopaedia Britannica, Inc., 1952 [1543]), p. 506.

[6] Paul D. MacLean, *The Triune Brain in Evolution: Role in Paleocerebral Functions*, (New York, NY: Springer Publishing, 1990).

[7] George Lakoff, *Thinking Points: Communicating Our American Values and Vision*, (New York, NY: Farrar, Straus, and Giroux, 2006), p. 38.

discover the truth; they create it. You'll read more about this type of emotionally-grounded thinking in the following chapters.

The conversations in this book approach topics from a gadfly perspective. Socrates was known by two metaphors: a gadfly and a midwife. As a gadfly, Socrates challenged many "truths" of the day that were based on assumptions or notions about reality. Many notions can be myth or fact, true or false. In today's political narratives, the frame is more important than actual fact. This may explain why a prominent national politician can feel safe in encouraging the voting public "to pass the bill [Obamacare] so you can know what's in it."

Socrates also saw his role as an educator to be similar to the role of a midwife--one who facilitates the birth of grand and noble ideas that can pollinate the world in creative ways. Notice, Socrates did not teach others what to think. He shaped their ability to think for themselves.

The primary objective of the conversations in this book is to challenge many of today's narratives, advanced by the political elite, consisting mostly of politicians, academics, journalists, and artists from Hollywood who believe others should buy or imitate what they create. If, in the process of presenting the analysis and reflections in these conversations, readers find alternative ways of seeing things, then this will be a nice outcome as well.

New understandings can liberate us from the chains of our illusions, described so eloquently by the cave allegory in Plato's *The Republic*.[8] Unfortunately, too many of our citizens are content to remain chained to illusions, because they are emotionally programmed to mistrust those trying to advance an alternate truth. We know who they are. Some reveal this form of bondage when they say: "let's agree to disagree."

Americans live in a perilous time. If a majority of the self-determining citizens of America do not stem the current drift of our Nation, they will discover the real consequences of their failure as cautioned by Hayek in *The Road to Serfdom* and documented by Hannah Arendt in her book, *The Origins of Totalitarianism*.[9]

---

[8] Plato, *The Dialogues of Plato* (Benjamin Jowett, Translator), in Robert. M. Hutchins (Ed.) Great Books of the Western Word, Volume 7, pp. 1-784, (Chicago, IL: Encyclopaedia Britannica, Inc., 1952), pp. 388-401.

[9] Hannah Arendt, *The Origins of Totalitarianism*, (New York, NY: Schocken Books, 2004 [1948]).

3 THE "INHERITED ECONOMY" NARRATIVE

August 16, 2012
O'Malley's Pub & Grill, Palmer Lake, Colorado

IM: Gadfly, I keep hearing one presidential candidate, who happens to be the incumbent, say he wants to "press forward" on his policies. He also says his opponent wants to return to past policies that got our nation into the trouble he's trying to fix. The voter has a choice to stay the current course or to regress.

Old Gadfly: What is your question?

IM: For whom should I vote?

Old Gadfly: Can you not think for yourself? What do you know about the situation?

IM: Except for *Fox News,* the *Wall Street Journal,* and a small handful of other news sources that seem to try to examine strengths and weaknesses of both candidates, most of the news networks, such as *ABC, CBS, NBC, CNN,* and *MSNBC,* and newspapers such as *The New York Times,* the *Los Angeles Times,* and *The Huffington Post,* and magazines such as *Time* and *Newsweek* seem pretty comfortable with the incumbent.

Old Gadfly: Yet, you seem to want a deeper understanding of which candidate has a better grasp on how to handle the economy. Let's think through this topic, the economy. What's wrong with it?

IM: I'd say there are two major problems: sustained high unemployment and increasing national debt.

Old Gadfly: O.K., let's focus on these problems for now. What do you think caused these problems?

IM: According to the prevailing public narrative, President George W. Bush policies got us into this mess. Some people refer to them as Bushonomics. Even the tax-exempt, nonpartisan think tank, The Center

for American Progress, published a white paper on it, *Understanding Bushonomics: How We Got into This Mess in the First Place*.[10] But, I found some issues with the paper (I think you and I will have a future conversation on this paper), and, when I tried to learn more about the Center at its website, I became very suspicious about the objectivity of the white paper. The description on the "About Us" page said, "We develop new policy ideas, critique the policy that stems from conservative values, challenge the media to cover the issues that truly matter, and shape the national debate."

Old Gadfly: What's disappointing about the statement?

IM: I have two concerns with it. First, while not all Americans embrace conservative values, as a liberal democracy we preach tolerance of different views, especially if they do not affect my individual liberty. Otherwise, we sacrifice some freedoms when policymakers impose values that stem from egalitarianism, which infringes upon some individual freedoms to promote equality as an outcome. Yet, this view of equality views people as objects as opposed to subjects. Second, challenging the media and shaping the national debate sounds like subtle encouragement of censorship or the unbridled tactic of engineering public sentiment (there will be a future conversation on engineering public sentiment). Also, it is an example of the "framing" you described in your monologue.

Old Gadfly: I do not disagree with your observations. But, let's get back to the economy and start with tax cuts. Since you are not a Copernican drone, I want you to do some analysis. One of the good things the federal government does is collect data.

- Go to the Internet and download the Fiscal Year 2013 Budget of the U.S. Government Historical Tables from the Office of Management and Budget.[11]

---

[10] Scott Lilly, *Understanding Bushonomics: How We Got into This Mess in the First Place* (White Paper), Center for American Progress, August 4, 2008. The white paper is available at http://www.americanprogress.org/issues/open-government/report/2008/08/04/4763/understanding-bushonomics/

[11] *The Fiscal Year 2013 Budget of the U. S. Government Historical Tables* publication is available at

- Now, go to Table 2.1 for tax revenue generated. Let's start building a database for the years 1987 through 2011.
- We will want to normalize the data to account for inflation and population growth. To adjust the revenue data for the years 1987 through 2011 in constant fiscal year 2011 dollars, use an inflation calculator such as the one available at the U.S. Department of Labor's Bureau of Labor Statistics.[12]
- For population growth, go to the US Census Bureau for the population data. Unfortunately, there is no single file that captures these data. There are three files: 1900 to 2002, 2003 to 2009, and projections for 2010 and 2011.[13]
- Let's identify the years that top marginal individual income tax rate changes were imposed. We can get these data from The Tax Policy Center, sponsored by the Urban Institute and The Brookings Institution.[14]
- Let's also include maximum long-term capital gains tax rates. This set of data is also available from the Tax Policy Center.[15]
- Finally, collect unemployment data from the Department of Labor's Bureau of Labor Statistics.[16]

IM: This seems like a lot to digest.

Old Gadfly: Let's just graph the individual income tax revenue in constant dollars per capita and unemployment rates between 1987 and 2011. Let the left hand axis reflect tax revenue and the right hand axis

---

http://www.whitehouse.gov/sites/default/files/omb/budget/fy2013/assets/hist.pdf

[12] The inflation calculator can be accessed at
http://www.bls.gov/data/inflation_calculator.htm

[13] The data for the years 1900 through 2002 are available at
http://www.census.gov/statab/hist/HS-01.pdf; data for the years 2003 through 2009 are available at
http://www.census.gov/popest/data/historical/2000s/vintage_ 2009/ index.html; and data for 2010 and 2011 are available at
http://www.census.gov/popest/data/national/ totals/ 2011/index.html

[14] Top marginal tax rate data are available at
http://www.taxpolicycenter.org/taxfacts/displayafact.cfm? Docid=213

[15] Long-term capital gain tax rate data are available at
http://www.taxpolicycenter.org/taxfacts/displayafact. cfm? Docid=161

[16] Unemployment data are available at
http://www.bls.gov/web/empsit/cpseea01.htm

indicate unemployment rates (inversed for easier comparison). The graph is illustrated in the next Figure.

IM: The graph shows increases and decreases. There seems to be a very close correspondence between employment rates and tax revenue generated.

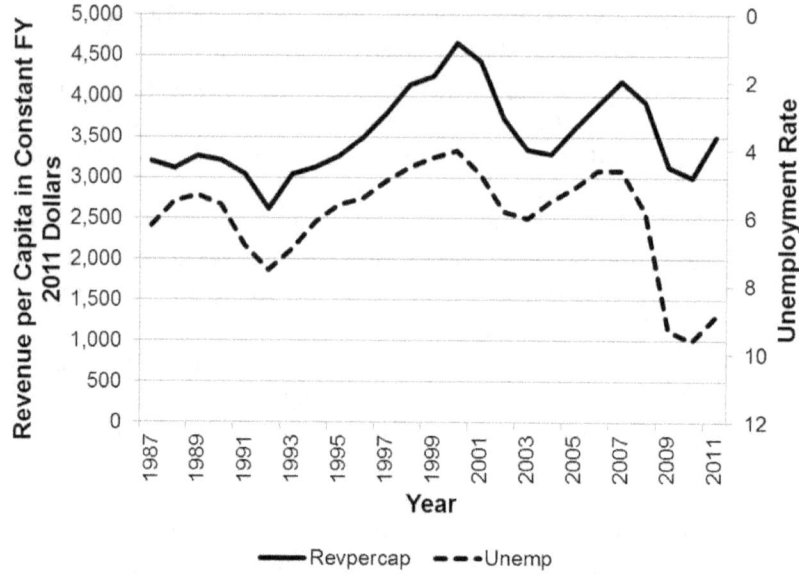

Figure 2. Tax Revenue per Capita and Unemployment Rates are Strongly Correlated between 1987 and 2011

Old Gadfly: This is correct, IM. Statistically, the correspondence is significant with a strong negative correlation coefficient of - .67.[17] As unemployment rates decrease revenue increases, and vice versa.

IM: So, there is a strong relationship between employment and revenue generated for government spending. Now, this leads to the question, how do tax rates effect employment or tax revenue?

Old Gadfly: Since Bush tax cuts, both top marginal tax rates and capital gains rates, are singled out by Democrats and progressives as causing the recession, let's position them on the graph to see what effect they had on revenue and unemployment rates. The next Figure shows what the graph looks like with tax rates superimposed.

---

[17] This coefficient is significant because the probability of this correspondence occurring through pure chance is well less than 1%. Additionally, a post-hoc power analysis of the data sample, using G*Power 3.1.5 software, reflects a strong population effect greater than .7 and a power of .995%.

IM: Bush took office in 2001. That year, top marginal tax rates were reduced by 1%. This change seemed to have had no effect on the sharp decline in employment and revenues following the recession stemming from the dot-com bubble burst.[18] Two years later, top marginal tax rates were reduced by 3.6% and capital gains tax rates were reduced by less than a percent. This seems to have slowed the unemployment rate and the loss of tax revenues. The following year, 2004, capital gains taxes were reduced by 5%. Unemployment rates improved from 6.0% in 2003 to 4.6% in 2007. Revenue per capita rose from $3,287 in 2004 to $4,185 in 2007. However, the year 2007 saw a sharp decline in employment rates and tax revenue, even though there were no tax rate changes.

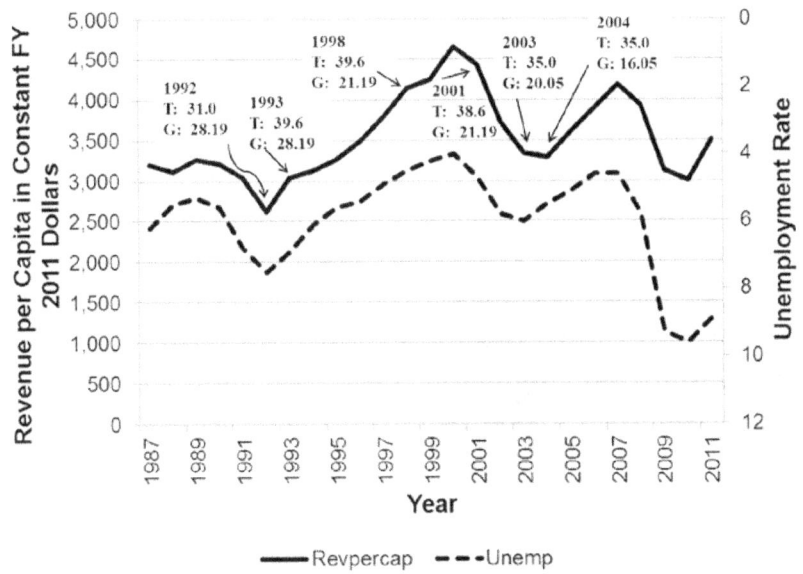

Figure 3. Changes in Top Marginal Tax Rates (T) and Capital Gain Tax Rates (C) in Comparison with Tax Revenue per Capita and Unemployment Rates between 1987 and 2011

     Old Gadfly: What happened in 2007?
     IM: What do you mean?
     Old Gadfly: Any changes in Congress?

---

[18] See "The Dot-Com Bubble Bursts," *The New York Times*, December 24, 2000, available at http://www. nytimes. com/2000/12/24/opinion/the-dot-com-bubble-bursts.html

IM: From 1994 through 2006, the Republican Party controlled both houses of Congress. In 2007, the Democrat Party achieved significant majorities in both houses of Congress.

Old Gadfly: Could political party dominance in Congress have an impact on employment? After all, the Democrat Party claims to be the advocate for labor.

IM: Your question addresses two separate points. First, political party matters when considering pro- or anti-business sentiment. Businesses generate jobs in the private sector. Senator Harry Reid, The Democratic

Majority Leader, received an 18% rating from the Chamber of Commerce in 2010.[19]

Congresswoman Nancy Pelosi, the Democratic Speaker of the House, received a 0% rating from the Chamber in 2010.[20] It is safe to say the two

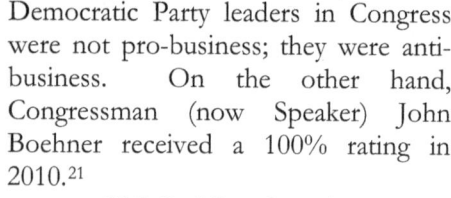

Democratic Party leaders in Congress were not pro-business; they were anti-business. On the other hand, Congressman (now Speaker) John Boehner received a 100% rating in 2010.[21]

Old Gadfly: So, what is your second point regarding labor?

IM: The second point involves two key concepts: employment and labor. Employment is a broader concept that includes employees that may or may not be affiliated with a union. To a Democrat or progressive, labor means an

---

[19] See Project Vote Smart data at
http://votesmart.org/candidate/evaluations/53320/harry-reid

[20] See Project Vote Smart data at
http://votesmart.org/candidate/evaluations/26732/nancy-pelosi

[21] See Project Vote Smart data at
http://votesmart.org/candidate/evaluations/27015/john-boehner

employee protected by union membership. Incidentally, only 7% of private sector employees are members of unions; whereas, over 36% of government employees, at the federal, state, and municipal levels are members of unions.

Old Gadfly: Are there any trends in the labor dynamics?

IM: Good question. Here is a table that summarizes trends between 1983 and 2010.

Table 1

Union Membership Patterns between 1983 and 2010

	1983	2010
Percent of Population	20.1%	11.9%
Percent of Private Sector	18.4%	6.9%
Percent of Public Sector	31.1%	36.2%

Note: Data is from the Bureau of Labor Statistics at http://www.bls.gov/news.release/ union2.toc.htm and the Economic History Association at http://eh.net/encyclopedia/article /friedman.unions.us

Old Gadfly: This is remarkable. The private sector has significantly reduced its need or desire for unions but the public sector, which one would think has no need for a union has continued to increase. Why do you think there has been such a significant change in these numbers?

IM: Private sector labor unions, which are heavily supported by political faction, have created a labor monopoly in some sectors, especially automobile manufacturing.[22] Unions in these sectors forced long-term contracts that made these companies less adaptive in a free market characterized by the need for rapid adaptation. Joseph Schumpeter's creative destruction theory explains why

---

[22] For a good analytical explanation of labor monopoly and its adverse consequences, see Thomas Friedman, *Capitalism and Freedom*, 40th Anniversary Edition, (Chicago, IL: University of Chicago Press, 2002 [originally published in 1962]), pp. 115-117, and 123-126.

these dynamics can destroy a company, or even an entire economy, in the long term.[23] Creative destruction essentially explains the industrial mutation that continuously revolutionizes the economic structure from within the economic system. In complex adaptive systems, this form of adaptation makes the system more complex yet more resilient and sustainable. I infer from this then that the tendency toward creative destruction is the nature of innovation and real progress in society.

Public sector unions are another factor. As the government grows in size, so does the power of public sector unions, again heavily supported by political faction. The lion's share of funding from the American Recovery and Reinvestment Act of 2009 subsidized public sector union affiliated payrolls in many of the States.[24] Any private sector subsidies that flowed from the Act targeted green industries, which aligned with political faction agendas. Little, if any, of the funding from the Act created long-term private sector jobs.

What is truly amazing is that governments and unions are rent-seekers. They depend upon others to pay for their existence. While they claim to create wealth, they can only distribute the wealth they take from those who actually create it. By the way, economic scholars explain that rent-seeking behavior actually reduces net social welfare because of the inherently wasteful use of resources in securing additional rent.[25] It is no coincidence that voting patterns and union demographics are very similar across our Nation.

Old Gadfly: What do you mean?

IM: If you look at the composition of red (Republican) and blue (Democrat) states in the 2008 presidential election, blue states generally clustered in the northeast and west coast. Red states clustered in the southeast and Midwest. Notice the union demographics in the following graphic.[26]

---

[23] Building upon Karl Marx's theory that capitalism initially generates wealth and then annihilates it, Joseph A. Schumpeter advances a more thoughtful explanation as a form of innovation in *Capitalism, Socialism and Democracy*, (New York, NY: Harper Perennial, 1942), pp. 81-86.

[24] The *lion's share* idiom, derived from several of Aesop's Fables, seems especially apropos for this discussion.

[25] For an interesting explanation of rent-seeking behavior and its adverse effect on an economy see John M. Levy, *Essential Microeconomics for Public Policy Analysis*, (Westport, CT: Praeger, 1995), pp. 96-99.

[26] The graphic is from the Bureau of Labor Statistics at http://www.bls.gov/news.release/union2.toc.htm

(U.S. rate = 11.9 percent)

Figure 4. Union Demographics in the United States
Source: U.S. Bureau of Labor Statistics

Old Gadfly: There does appear to be an alignment between union presence and voting patterns.

IM: We seemed to have digressed somewhat from our discussion on tax rate changes and their effect on unemployment rates and tax revenue.

Old Gadfly: Not really. Too many people are too eager to overly simplify the picture. Your discussion on labor and unions is an important element in explaining dynamics that shape our overall economy. For example, in Figure 3, there is a reversal of trends for both revenue and unemployment rates in 2010. Were there any known changes to account for this trend?

IM: There were no tax rate changes, but the Senate lost some seats to Republicans and Republicans gained a significant majority in the House of Representatives.

Old Gadfly: Your observations seem to align with your implication about political parties and their effect on business in the private sector. In the final analysis, do your findings prove anything?

IM: Technically, no. However, aside from a preponderance of public narrative rhetoric, there is no evidence that Bush tax cuts caused the recession; yet, from our analysis, I conclude that a strong argument can be made that the anti-business Democrat Party had a chilling effect on private sector business, starting in 2007. The private sector significantly reduced capital investments that otherwise could have increased jobs, reducing the unemployment rate and a corresponding loss of tax revenues.

Old Gadfly: Then why does Obama keep saying he inherited a recession caused by Bush policies?

IM: Perhaps to deflect attention from the real causes.

Old Gadfly: We covered a lot in this conversation, and perhaps, in the process, uncovered a more accurate picture. Let's address the debt issue in our next one.

4 TAXES, UNEMPLOYMENT, AND PUBLIC DEBT

August 27, 2012
The Coffee Cup Café, Monument, Colorado

IM: Gadfly, in our last conversation, we did some analysis regarding causes for the economic problem that President Obama and many others attribute to Bush policies. In particular, we looked at tax cuts. I was amazed that with some simple analysis of federal government data, *there is no evidence to conclude the Bush era tax cuts had a causal effect on the apparent recession* that Obama complains about inheriting.

Old Gadfly: I agree, IM. Nonetheless, how do you respond to those, especially President Obama, who claim, the federal government can't afford to pay for tax cuts for the wealthy?[27] On April 13, 2011, Obama said (see Appendix A for the entire speech):

> After Democrats and Republicans committed to fiscal discipline during the 1990s, we lost our way in the decade that followed. We increased spending dramatically for two wars and an expensive prescription drug program — but we didn't pay for any of this new spending. Instead, we made the problem worse with trillions of dollars in unpaid-for tax cuts — tax cuts that went to every millionaire and billionaire in the country.

---

[27] See "The Tax Cut 'Giveaway' and Criticizing Comments by Unnamed Advisors—Today's Q's for O's WH, 7/26/12," *ABC News*, July 26, 2012, available at http://abcnews.go.com/blogs/politics/2012/07/the-tax-cut-giveaway-and-criticizing-comments-by-unnamed-advisers-todays-qs-for-os-wh-72612/

Notice, President Obama clearly believes the government **gave** money "to every millionaire and billionaire in the country."[28] The implication is that this was money that could not be spent on the cost of government, leading to annual deficit spending and an accumulating public debt.

IM: Amazingly, while Democrats and progressives push for higher tax rates on the wealthy, the assumption is that this fiscal policy will increase tax revenue over all. What Democrats and progressives also assume is that employment rates will remain constant during this time.

Old Gadfly: And, as we know from our last discussion, unemployment rose significantly between 2007 and 2010, while revenue dropped significantly. The evidence clearly indicates unemployment rates have a strong, statistically significant negative correlation with tax revenue generated.[29] Yet, Obama and his progressive cohorts keep their focus on raising taxes on the wealthy to meet federal government spending desires instead of what it would take to increase jobs in the private sector. Why do you think the answer to this question is important?

IM: Good question, Gadfly. The answer is simple: Governments do not generate income—private sector corporations and individuals generate income through capital investment and labor-related production. It is the private sector where wealth is created. Even those who work for the government, like President Obama, may earn an income, but it is paid for in tax revenue from the wealth creators. While Democrats and progressives like to claim the government is "giving" benefits, the "giving" generally costs money and that money comes from the private sector. To suggest that the government is paying money to millionaires and billionaires completely dismisses the reality that a government is funded by tax revenue--money that is generated by businesses and financial institutions in

---

[28] For a good explanation on the Bush tax cuts and project costs and surpluses, see Glenn Kessler, "Revisiting the Cost of the Bush Tax Cuts," *The Washington Post*, May 10, 2011, available at http://www.washingtonpost.com/ blogs/fact-checker/post/revisiting-the-cost-of-the-bush-tax-cuts/2011/05/09/AFxTFtbG_blog.html

[29] A two-tailed, Pearson correlation coefficient of $r = -.67, p < .01$.

the private sector. But, and this is the sad part, Democrats and progressives seek rent so that they can in turn distribute it to those they determine should receive it. We call this redistributing the wealth. A modern day Robin Hood would be taking the resources the federal government has seized through fiscal policy in order to return it to those who produced those resources.

Old Gadfly: Great points, IM. Let's get back to our analysis. If the Bush tax cuts cannot be blamed on the government spending deficits and growing public debt, then are there other explanations?

IM: As opposed to tax rates, I think the focus of our analysis should be the amount of government spending.

Old Gadfly: How can we analyze government spending as a factor related to the health of our economy?

IM: In preparation for today's conversation, I already conducted some analysis. For this phase, I collected public domain data on annual federal government spending listed as outlays and annual surplus/deficits between 1987 and 2011. This data was in Table 1.1 in the Fiscal Year 2013 Budget of the U.S. Government Historical Tables from the Office of Management and Budget.[30] I used the same unemployment data from the Department of Labor's Bureau of Labor Statistics.

Old Gadfly: What did you discover?

IM: The graph (see below) shows a comparison between annual unemployment rates and annual surpluses or deficits. The left vertical axis represents surpluses or deficits, and the right vertical axis represents unemployment rates, on an inverted scale. The graph clearly indicates that, assuming all things being equal, if unemployment increases, so will government spending deficits. To the contrary, as unemployment decreases, so do spending deficits. I also ran a Pearson correlation statistical test with these two variables and found an even stronger negative correlation.[31] Even more astonishing, a regression analysis revealed that unemployment rates explain 86% of the variation in annual surpluses or deficits.[32]

---

[30] *The Fiscal Year 2013 Budget of the U. S. Government Historical Tables* publication is available at
http://www.whitehouse.gov/sites/default/files/omb/budget/fy2013/assets/hist.pdf

[31] A two-tailed Pearson correlation coefficient of $r = -.93$, $p < .0001$.

[32] A bivariate regression analysis revealed an $R^2 = .857$, $F(1, 23) = 145.147$, $p = 000$. A Durbin-Watson test confirmed some lag effect in the time-series evaluation, which is to be expected but not to such an extent as to invalidate the findings.

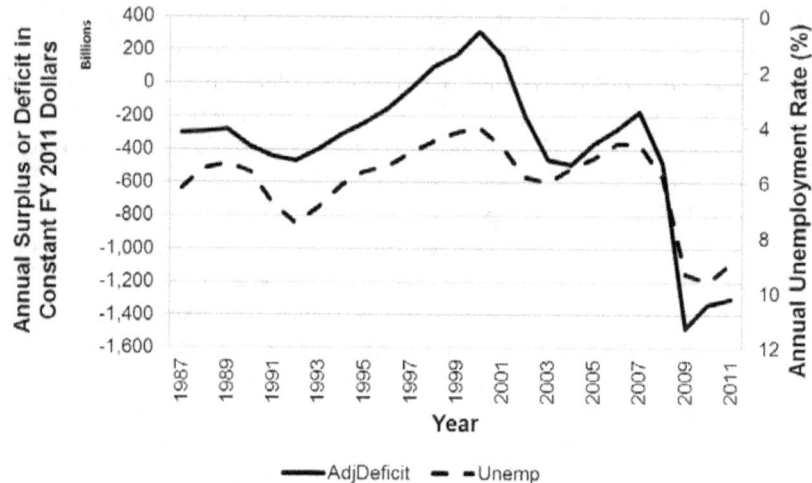

Figure 5. Correlation between Annual Unemployment Rates and Government Deficits between 1987 and 2011

Old Gadfly: Impressive, IM. Let me see if I understand what your analysis is telling me. When you say unemployment rates explain 86% of annual surplus or deficit spending amounts, are you saying that only 14% of the explanation comes from other factors?

IM: Yes.

Old Gadfly: What could some of those factors be?

IM: It's hard to say. Some of the factors could be related to union behavior, fiscal policy (i.e., individual and corporate tax rates) that influences the extent of outsourcing, or international trade dynamics. Look what happened to Eduardo Saverin, the Facebook co-founder, who decided to move to Singapore.[33] Saverin responded to a lot of criticism when he announced he was moving to Singapore. He claims to have paid millions in taxes. Ironically, Saverin is originally from Brazil; yet, he has elected to move to Singapore, which will drastically reduce his tax liability on future earnings because there are no capital gains taxes.[34]

---

[33] Jim Puzzanghera, "Facebook Co-founder Says He's Grateful and Has Paid Taxes," *The Los Angeles Times*, May 17, 2012, available at http://articles.latimes.com/2012/may/17/business/la-fi-mo-saverin-facebook-taxes-20120517

[34] See Jim Puzzanghera, "Senators Want to Stop Facebook Co-founder from Dodging Taxes," *The Los Angeles Times*, May 17, 2012, available at http://articles.latimes.com/2012/may/17/business/la-fi-mo-facebook-saverin-taxes-20120517

Old Gadfly: It amazes me that the media has not sought out this kind of information to sufficiently inform the public that it serves. But, let's get back to jobs. Help me to understand something. President Obama says that his Administration created 4.5 million jobs in the private sector in the 29 months leading up to today's conversation (see the graph below).[35] That sounds like an achievement. And it seems to correspond with a slight reduction in deficit spending between 2010 and 2011: from -1.334 trillion to -1.300 trillion.

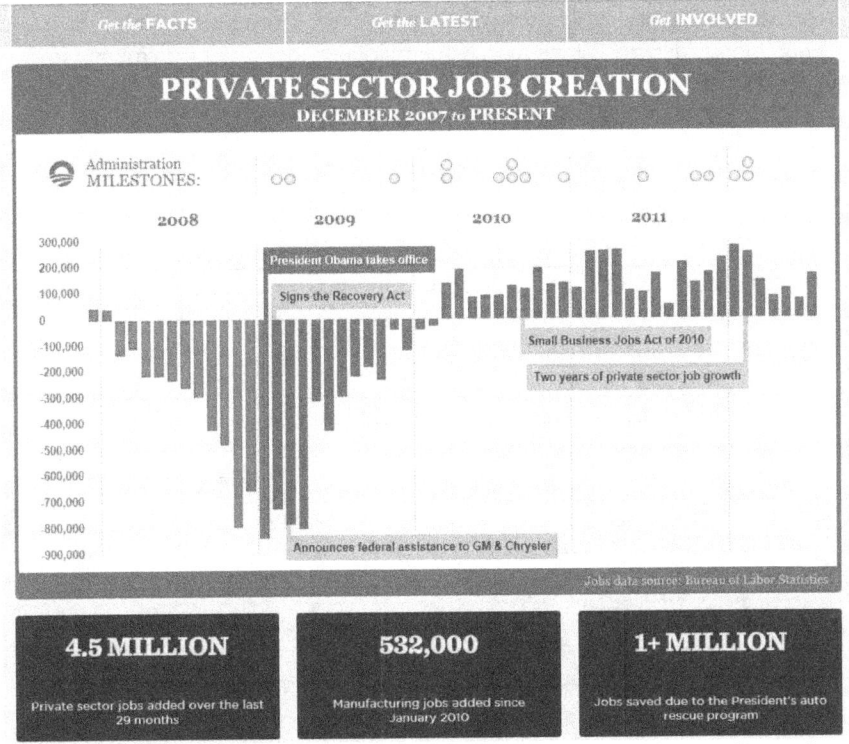

Figure 6. Job Creation Graphic Published on the Obama Campaign Website
Source: http://www.barackobama.com/jobsrecord/

IM: All I can say is the Obama campaign graph is a classic example of "lies, damned lies, and statistics."[36]
Old Gadfly: Why do you make such a claim?

---

[35] This graphic was retrieved from http://www.barackobama.com/jobsrecord/

[36] For an interesting discussion on the origin of this quotation, "lies, damned lies, and statistics, see http://www. york.ac.uk/depts/maths/histstat/lies.htm

IM: Because I have looked into the data from the Bureau of Labor Statistics and arrived at a completely different picture of reality.

Old Gadfly: IM, you impress me with the quality of your sense of discernment, unlike the Copernican drones I described in the opening chapter to this book. Tell me more about your analysis.

IM: Since 1977, the lowest unemployment rate was 4.0% in 2000. The public narrative does not credit six years, between 1994 and 2000, of a Republican-led Congress that insisted upon balancing the federal budget and welfare reform that moved many unemployed individuals into the workforce. As we have already discussed, the dot-com bubble burst and other factors led to a recession with rising annual unemployment rates of 4.7%, 5.8%, and 6.0% for the years 2001, 2002, and 2003, respectively. Also, recall in our last conversation, we discussed how the Bush Administration called for income tax and capital gains tax cuts across the board (not just for the wealthy). Consequently, in 2004, unemployment rates began to improve: 5.5% in 2004, 5.1% in 2005, 4.6% in 2006, and 4.6% in 2007. The resulting improved unemployment rates had two beneficial effects: an increase in individual tax revenues generated--that is, $3,287 per capita in 2004 compared to $4,185 per capita in 2007; and a reduction in federal spending deficits--that is, $491 billion in 2004 compared to $174 billion in 2007.

Old Gadfly: I still do not see why you refer to the Obama claim as "lies, damned lies, and statistics."

IM: Let's take a look at the raw data from the Bureau of Labor Statistics. There are certain data points we should consider: 2003, 2007, 2008, 2009, 2010, and 2011.

- The year 2003 is important because it represents the peak of the recession President Bush inherited.
- The year 2007 is important because the Democrat Party gained significant majorities in both Houses of Congress.
- The year 2008 represents President Bush's last year in office.
- Starting with the year 2009, the Democrat Party controlled the Executive and Legislative branches of government.
- The year 2010 is important because it was the last year the Democrat Party controlled the White House and both Houses of Congress.
- Finally, the year 2011 is important because it represents the year the Republican Party took control of the House of Representatives.

To simplify the discussion, I created a chart to demonstrate what actually happened regarding jobs lost and gained during the years mentioned above.

Old Gadfly: What do you conclude from this data?

IM: First of all, I cannot determine how the claim "4.5 million jobs created" comes from. An old friend of mine once told me that the Mayor of Phoenix boasted about the large population increases taking place during his tenure in office; but, what he failed to tell the public is that for every five people that moved to Phoenix, three moved away. think this may be a good analogy. Somehow, the Obama Administration seems to count new jobs gained, but does not count jobs lost. Secondly, if you simply calculate the net jobs gained or lost between Bush's last year in office from the number employed at the end of 2011, the number is 5,493,000 fewer Americans employed in the private sector. This is a significant loss of jobs, not a gain. Now, if you use the Bureau of Labor Statistics figure for the number employed in July 2012, which does not reflect what will be reported as the annual unemployment rate for the entire year 2012, the number employed is 142,220,000. This calculation still represents a net loss of 3,142,000 jobs between the end of 2008 and the end of July 2012. A net loss of over 3 million jobs is not what the Obama Administration wants to admit. Thus, they advance lies and damned lies under the cloak of manufactured statistics.

Table 2

Comparisons between Employment, Unemployment, and Party Affiliation of the President, Senate, and House of Representatives for the Years 2003, and 2007 through 2012

Year	Employed	Unemployment Rate (%)	Net Gain (+) Loss (-)	President	Senate	House
2003	137,736,000	6.0	N/A	Rep	Rep	Rep
2007	146,047,000	4.6	8,311,000	Rep	Dem	Dem
2008	145,362,000	5.8	-685,000	Rep	Dem	Dem
2009	139,877,000	9.3	-5,485,000	Dem	Dem	Dem
2010	139,064,000	9.6	-813,000	Dem	Dem	Dem
2011	139,869,000	8.9	805,000	Dem	Dem	Rep
2012	142,101,000[a]	8.1	2,232,000	Dem	Dem	Rep

Note. [a]The number employed is as of August 2012 from the Bureau of Labor Statistics, retrieved from
http://www.bls.gov/news.release/archives/empsit_09072012.pdf

Old Gadfly: But when the Obama campaign claims 4.5 million jobs in the past 29 months, it looks like they don't want us to look at the number employed after Obama's first year in office. By using the end of 2010 figure of 139,064,000 employed and the July 2012 figure of 142,220,000, there seems to be a net gain of 3,156,000 employees.

IM: I agree. So, even if you manipulate the numbers this way, the Obama campaign claim is still over 1.3 million more than what the actual data reveals. Quite frankly, for two years, President Bush had to contend with a hostile, anti-business Democratic Congress. So, it is disingenuous to disregard data earlier than 2010. Also disingenuous is the manner in which the Obama Administration plays down the growth in federal sector jobs. In their recent budget, the Administration admits to a "slight increase" in nonmilitary federal jobs, from 1.9 million in 2008 to 2.1 million in 2010, explained on p. 9 of the Historical Budget Tables for 2012.[37] This "slight increase" represents a 10.5% expansion of federal government jobs, when unemployment rates in the private sector have ranged from 8.2% to nearly 10%.

Old Gadfly: I see what you mean. So far, we have talked about tax cuts and unemployment rates in relation to government spending deficits. Do you have any insights on other factors that explain how the deficits contributed to our public debt?

IM: Absolutely. There are two other major factors to consider: one is party affiliation and the other is type of spending. For the first factor, I was not surprised to see that party affiliation has been fairly even for the Office of the President between 1933 and 2012; but Democrats have dominated more so in in the Senate and House of Representatives. The following table summarizes the demographics.

Table 3

Distribution of Political Power in Terms of Years in Control of the Office of the Presidency, Senate, and House of Representatives

President		Senate		House	
Dem	Rep	Dem	Rep	Dem	Rep
44	36	57.5	22.5	62	18

---

[37] *The Fiscal Year 2012 Budget of the U. S. Government Historical Tables* publication is available at http://www.whitehouse.gov/sites/default/files/omb/budget/fy2012/assets/hist.pdf, p. 9.

Old Gadfly: These numbers show a significant difference in party dominance in Washington, D. C.

IM: This table really does not demonstrate the difference. I was shocked to see how lopsided political party dominance has been in terms of Congressional demographics when I mapped the differences in a graphic. The following graphic (see Figure 7) depicts the magnitude of party dominance in Congress between 1933 and 2012. Republican dominance is reflected in the area above zero. Democratic dominance is reflected in the area below zero (for a description of the algorithm I employed in calculating party dominance, see Appendix B). As you can see, Republicans have rarely dominated Congress, and even during these short periods the magnitude was low. The most significant era of Republican dominance was between 1994 and 2006. As we know, the greatest surpluses during this period were generated between 1994 and 2000. Sometimes I believe we place far too much emphasis on the President when it is Congress that is charged by the Constitution to regulate annual budgets.

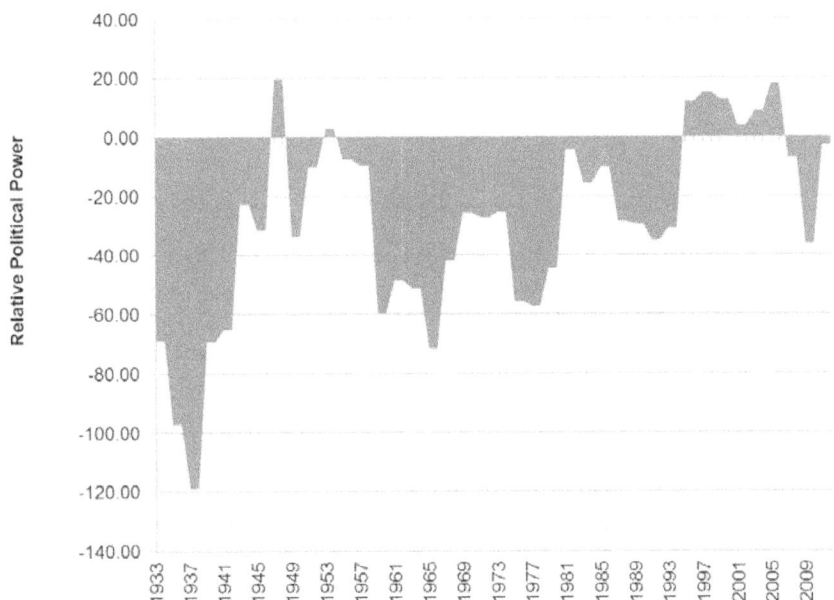

Figure 7. Relative Political Power in Congress between 1933 and 2012

Old Gadfly: IM, I can see why you identified party affiliation as the first of the two factors regarding government spending. How do you explain the second factor—the type of spending?

IM: The most significant factor in this entire discussion is government spending. We hear a lot about tax cuts, unemployment, and deficits; but, the real issue is government spending. Keep in mind that while the Constitution requires Congress to pass a government budget, there has been no congressionally approved budget during President Obama's entire tenure, even with a Democrat-controlled Congress. My next chart depicts government spending (left vertical scale) between 1987 and 2011 in constant 2011 dollars. The right vertical scale reflects spending for human resources (i.e., entitlements controlled by the Department of Health and Human Services) and defense (Department of Defense).

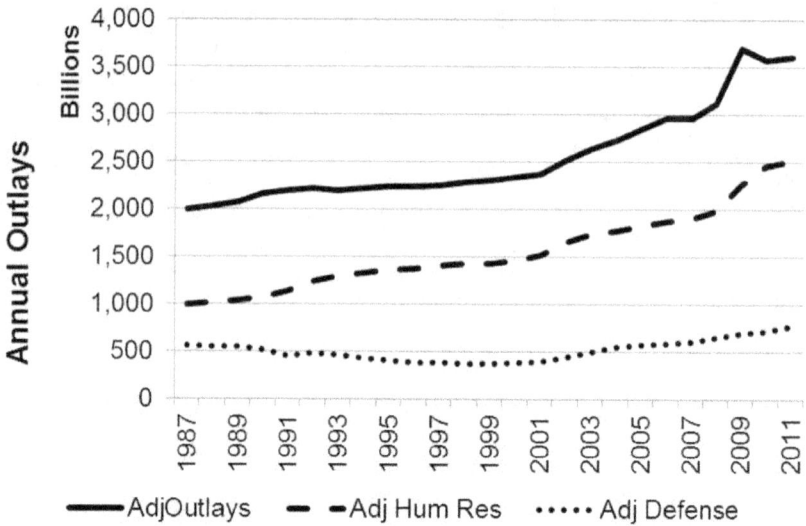

Figure 8. Total Federal Outlays, Human Resource Outlays, and Defense Outlays between 1987 and 2011

As you can see, defense spending has only increased by about $250 billion over 1987 outlays, while human resource entitlement spending has risen significantly by $1.5 trillion and clearly accounts for the lion's share of extra government spending. Keep in mind; these numbers have been adjusted for population growth and inflation.

Old Gadfly: It looks like most of government's human resources spending is linked to entitlements, and in 2011 our government spent approximately 2.5 trillion dollars on these entitlements. This reality reflects why Niall Ferguson recently described the direction as "Obama's America," where half the population pays no federal taxes, and, where at least one member per household in this same half of the population receives at least one type of government benefit.[38] Ferguson also said America is becoming a 50–50 nation: half pay taxes, the other half receive benefits.[39]

---

[38] Niall Ferguson, "Niall Ferguson: Obama's Gotta Go," *Newsweek*, August 19, 2012. The article is available at

IM: And in the process of pandering to an entitlement class for political purposes, the Obama Administration has put our nation at grave risk. Even after adjusting for population growth and inflation, the cost of the federal government in 1933 was $630 per person; at the end of 2011, the cost was nearly $12,000 per person. Think about it: for a family of four, the federal income tax liability is $48,000 per year. Also, after accounting for inflation and population growth, the Bush Administration added 3.08 trillion dollars to the public debt over an eight year period. In just three years of his first term, President Obama added 5.04 trillion dollars to the public debt. Look at Figure 7 and the steep rise in federal outlays in 2009. So, there is no doubt that Obama has sharply increased government spending. As we know, in our own households, we try to keep our expenses below our own revenue streams; otherwise, we accumulate debt.

Old Gadfly: Good analysis, IM. Can you now synthesize what we have discussed in terms of the connections between taxes, unemployment, and public debt?

IM: In this case, the real unit of analysis is the federal government. If we treat the federal government as a person who makes choices by weighing values against risk, then we might better understand the nature of the problem. President Obama and progressives currently exercising political power represent this person. Values represent progressive views of a powerful central government that ensure social justice and equality in outcomes. This is why we hear Obama and progressives use expressions such as "paying one's fair share." The risk is losing power through elections.

Now, with this as the context, Obama must push for a strong central government, which needs more and more resources, that is, tax revenue. That's the real focus. This money is critical for making sure the central government can redistribute wealth for equality purposes. The only real control Obama and progressives have in this regard is to demand more rent, that is, tax revenue. In their view, it would be socially unjust to demand rent from those who have less to give. Explained this way, it seems Obama and progressives are looking out for others. Yet, the real moral issue is when is it right to coercively take from some to give to others? This dilemma highlights the critical balance between liberty and egalitarianism. It also sheds light on how naïve the progressive approach is in "taking care" of those in need. The progressive approach completely

---

http://www.thedailybeast.com/newsweek/2012/08/19/niall-ferguson-on-why-barack-obama-needs-to-go.html

[39] Ibid.

dismisses the innovative talent and caring sentiment that already exists outside of the halls of government.

Without a sincere attempt to "partner" with business leaders in the private sector, our political elites, literally represented by President Obama, demand more rent from those who could actually solve the problem. Tax increases take money out of the private sector that could be used for investment and new jobs. When unemployment rates decline, overall tax revenues increase. When unemployment rates rise, overall tax revenues decrease, placing a larger demand on government resources in the form of unemployment benefits, food stamps, and so forth. The latter increases annual deficits and the public debt.

Old Gadfly: It all still seems so abstract.

IM: I agree Gadfly. And, if it is difficult for discerning minds such as yours and mine to comprehend, then imagine how difficult it is for Copernican drones. In an attempt to make the employment dynamic less abstract, I built the following matrix (See Table 4) for a simple comparison of the benefits and costs of jobs gained or lost in the private and public sectors. Just for clarification, public sector means the government. There are significant differences.

Old Gadfly: The comparison clearly demonstrates the importance of private sector jobs and the adverse effect of a growing government. Jobs provide strategic leverage against deficits and debt accumulation and additional tax revenue for government costs. Whereas, a very short-sighted emphasis on tax rate increases does absolutely nothing to create private sector jobs. And when the tax rate increases are intended to cover the cost of a growing government, they generate a negative compounding effect, where the debt burden increases in a nonlinear fashion.

IM: Unfortunately, Gadfly, that is exactly what we see playing out with a dominant progressive faction in Washington.

Old Gadfly: So, does your analysis indicate any political party effect on the connections between taxes, unemployment, and public debt?

IM: Absolutely. Bush, a Republican President with a Republican Congress mitigated the effect of the recession they inherited in 2001 by lowering top marginal tax rates, which in turn improved unemployment rates and net tax revenues. Yet, I do not recall either the President or any Republican members of Congress complaining about "the recession they inherited." They simply collaborated with business leaders in the private sector to get our economy back on track by keeping earned income, with lower tax rates to grow jobs. On the other hand, look what happened in 2007. Democrats enjoyed large majorities in both houses of Congress. With no tax rate changes, unemployment rose sharply, tax revenues dropped significantly. With government spending rising sharply and tax revenues declining, the government incurred increasing deficits, adding more public debt.

Table 4

Comparison of Benefits and Costs of Private and Public Sector Job Gains and Losses

Jobs Gain/Loss	Benefit	Cost
Private		

Job Gain	• Self esteem
	• Productivity (wealth creation)
	  o Increased consumption
	  o Increased savings
	• Tax revenue
		• None

Job Loss	• None	• Loss of self esteem
		• Loss of productivity (wealth)
		  o Reduced consumption
		  o Depleted savings
		• Loss of tax revenue
		• Unemployment compensation (adds to deficit)
		• Debt to offset deficit

Public		
Job Gain	• Self esteem	• Loss of private sector productivity (loss of wealth creation) • Added overhead cost, requires an increase in tax resources • Increased taxation need reduces private sector job creation
Job Loss	• Additional resource available for private sector production (wealth creation) • Less overhead cost/burden on tax payers	• None

Old Gadfly: The charts we've discussed clearly reflect the effect of the Democrat worldview that the government controls the economy and must therefore control private sector business through stifling regulation. This view has not inspired the private sector to invest cash reserves into expanding business and the jobs that would be created in the process. Despite claims to the contrary, Republicans are not anti-government or anti-tax; they are for limited government and reasonable taxation.

IM: Perhaps in a future conversation we can discuss how Democratic politicians, in collaboration with a liberal media, shaped a public narrative to demonize President Bush and by affiliation the Republican Party.

Old Gadfly: It appears the politically manufactured public narrative between 2001 and 2006 accounted for the major shift toward a Democratic Congress in 2007, with some of that momentum carrying over to the presidential campaign in 2008. This has been a very enlightening conversation, IM. But, before we bring it to an end, I must say the most encouraging phase on your tax revenue graphic (see Figure 3), discussed in our last conversation, seems to be during the 1992 to 2000 timeframe. How would you account for this dynamic?

IM: I have always read and heard that this good news picture was President Clinton's handiwork. Yet, based on my own critical analysis of the situation, I think President Clinton demonstrated what an excellent surfer he was when he brilliantly anticipated the economic wave being generated by other factors and still claims credit for the "strong economy of the 90s."

Old Gadfly: This topic seems to be taking us away from today's theme about taxes, unemployment, and public debt. Let's start our next conversation with your assessment of President Clinton's talent for economic surfing. Until then, keep in mind that also we want our discussion to relate to today's contest regarding political visions for America.

IM: That sounds like a good plan, Gadfly. I also want us to eventually talk about some other topics that we've touched upon in our conversations, such as: a manufactured public narrative, the Center for American Progress's white paper on Bushonomics, the housing crisis, and financial sector deregulation.

Old Gadfly: Let's plan on it. Thank you for the wonderful discussion, IM. I'm ready for a glass of wine.

5 THE ART OF ECONOMY SURFING

September 7, 2012
Serrano's Coffee, Monument, Colorado

IM: Gadfly, before we get into our discussion about former President Clinton's economy surfing skills, are there any additional points we may have left out of our discussion on taxes, unemployment, and national debt?

Old Gadfly: I took another look at the claim of 4.5 million jobs created by the Obama Administration in the past 29 months. As you recall, we concluded this number does not add up. Perhaps the claim fails what former President Clinton called "an arithmetic test" in his policy lecture at the Democratic National Convention

(DNC; Wednesday, September 5, 2012).[40] Nonetheless, we wondered why the period did not start in January of 2009, the beginning of the Obama Administration. By starting at that point, the employment situation would

---

[40] For an interesting news article on former President Clinton's Slick Willie reputation, see Rupert Cornwell, "Slick Willie: Clinton's Untold Story," *The Independent*, September 23, 2009, available at http://www. independent. co.uk/news/world/americas/slick-willie-clintons-untold-story-1791711.html

still show a net loss of 3.1 million jobs. What change took place between January 2009 and July 2012? There was no change in top marginal tax rates. But, in November 2010, there was a political sea change in Congress, especially the House of Representatives. So, I looked at the unemployment rates for this period and discovered the unemployment rate trend reversed when Republicans took control of the House.[41] The number of unemployed at the end of 2010 was 14,825,000. The number of unemployed in July 2012 was 12,794,000, a net gain of a little more than 2 million jobs.

IM: Yet, former President Clinton alleged in his DNC lecture that Obama created 4.5 million jobs. Should we believe him?

Old Gadfly: I remember when Clinton looked into the camera and said, "I did not have sexual relations with that woman," and then later was found guilty of perjury by a grand jury, and faced impeachment proceedings in Congress.[42]

IM: What happened with the impeachment?

Old Gadfly: In accordance with an established process, the House of Representatives, controlled by Republicans, brought impeachment charges against Clinton, similar to an indictment in other criminal court proceedings. The impeachment charge then moved to the Senate for the actual trial, where conviction or acquittal would take place. Clinton was acquitted of the impeachment charges (this did not mean exoneration), because the Senate was controlled by the Democratic Party; not a single Democrat voted against Clinton.

IM: Perhaps he has redeemed himself in terms of honesty.

Old Gadfly: Clinton spent a lot of time during his DNC lecture bragging about all the great things he did for the economy while President. Yet, he did not share any of the credit for "his successes" with a Republican dominated Congress, which drove a balanced budget and the welfare reform that put a lot of Americans in the workforce.[43] While taking credit

---

[41] For the actual unemployment rates, see Bureau of Labor Statistics data at http://www.bls.gov/web/empsit/ cpseea01.htm

[42] For a YouTube recording of former President Clinton denying he had sex with Monica Lewinsky see http://www.youtube.com/watch?v=KiIP_KDQmXs; for an explanation of the perjury charge against former President Clinton, see "What Is Clinton's Perjury Defense?" *Slate*, December 18, 1998, available at http://www.slate.com/articles/news_and_politics/explainer/1998/12/what_is_clintons_perjury_defense.html

[43] The welfare reform stemmed from Personal Responsibility and Public Law 104-193, Work Opportunity Reconciliation Act of 1996. The complete text of the Act is available at http://www.gpo.gov/fdsys/pkg/PLAW-104publ193/pdf/PLAW-104publ193.pdf

for many imagined successes, Clinton seemed to overlook the recession George Bush inherited.

IM: But, I was impressed by all the facts included in Clinton's speech.

Old Gadfly: Clinton threw out a lot of *numbers* at the DNC to fit the Obama narrative or "frame." Numbers are not necessarily facts. The problem with a lot of Clinton's *facts* is that they lacked the proper context. Let me describe two examples. First, Clinton said, since "1961, the Republicans have held the White House 28 years, the Democrats 24. In those 52 years, our economy produced 66 million private sector jobs. What's the jobs score? Republicans 24 million, Democrats 42 million." Clinton clearly implied by this statement that Democratic Presidents have been far more successful than Republican presidents in creating private sector jobs.

IM: So, how is he wrong?

Old Gadfly: First, employment is a cyclic dynamic. A person who takes on a job in January, but loses it by December, is a net zero jobs gained. Let's take a broader look at the relationship between political party and employment. We're going to actually examine this issue using federal government data and robust statistical analysis. We have employment data from 1933 through 2011. We also know not only which party occupied the white house, but to what degree party dominated both houses of Congress (see Appendix B). The Labor Department's Bureau of labor Statistics estimates a variety of employment circumstances, such as percent of the employable population that is employed and the percent of the population that is unemployed, based on those filing for unemployment compensation. As a common measure of the health of our economy, we typically look at the percent of unemployed. So, how can we determine whether Clinton's numbers reflect any semblance of fact? I'll explain.

The following table presents correlations between (a) party affiliation of the President, degree of party dominance in the House of Representatives, degree of party dominance for the Senate, an aggregate degree of party dominance in Congress, and an aggregate degree of party dominance for the white house and Congress combined; and (b) unemployment rates. The correlations represent three different periods: 1933 through 2011, 1933 through 1960, and 1961 through 2011. The latter period is what Clinton focused on in his DNC speech.

IM: There are remarkable distinctions in these correlations. The entire period between 1933 and 2011 shows strong negative correlations in all five categories reflecting party affiliation. And it is obvious that the period between 1933 and 1960 skewed these correlations for the entire period, with little to not statistically significant correlations between 1961 and 2011.

Old Gadfly: I agree with your assessment. Now, what does the negative correlation tell you? Remember, in our analysis during the last conversation we mapped out degree of party affiliation for congress between 1933 and 2011. Democratic numbers were in the negative range; and Republic numbers were in the positive range. Also, keep in mind that as unemployment rates increase, the values become more positive, that, is from zero to a positive number, such as 4% or 7% unemployed.

Table 5

Correlations between Unemployment Rates and Party Affiliation in the Executive and Legislative Branches of the Federal Government

Federal Branches	1933-2011		1933-1960		1961-2011	
President	-.194	*	-.328	*	.120	
Senate	-.498	**	-.678	**	.074	
House	-.649	**	-.813	**	-.274	*
Congress	-.604	**	-.778	**	-.101	
President and Congress	-.337	**	-.540	**	.087	

Note. $* p < .10; ** p < .01.$

IM: Based on how the numbers are calculated, if party affiliation *increased* its strength to the *left*, that is Democrat, with a corresponding *increase* in unemployment rates, the correlation would be *negative*. On the other hand, if party affiliation *increased* its strength to the *left*, with a corresponding *decrease* in unemployment rates, the correlation would be *positive*.

Old Gadfly: That is correct, IM. So, based on how the statistical correlation analysis portrays the actual data, which political party corresponded to better unemployment rates?

IM: As the Democratic Party lost its overwhelming dominance in Congress, which meant more Republicans in Congress, the overall employment condition improved. The data for 1961 through 2011 is far less compelling, perhaps because the Democratic Party lost even more dominance in Congress; yet the only correlation of slight statistical significance was for the House of Representatives with a moderate negative correlation. This value still indicates as political power shifted to the right with more Republicans, unemployment rates improved.

Old Gadfly: Excellent analysis, IM. Does the following graphic (Figure 9) reflect the analysis?

IM: Yes. The statistical analysis clearly does not support Clinton's story.

Old Gadfly: Now, let me address another Clinton *fact* in his DNC speech. Clinton said, "In the last 29 months the economy has produced about 4.5 million private sector jobs. But last year, the Republicans blocked the president's jobs plan costing the economy more than a million new jobs. So here's another jobs score: President Obama plus 4.5 million, congressional Republicans zero." As you know, IM, we have already talked about these numbers. Do you remember the data in Table 2 from our last conversation?

IM: Yes, at the end of President Bush's term, there were 145,362,000 people employed. At the end of Obama's first year, there were 5,485,000 fewer people working. Since then 3,261,000 people have returned to work. This does not look like the 4.5 million jobs that Clinton and Obama keep declaring.

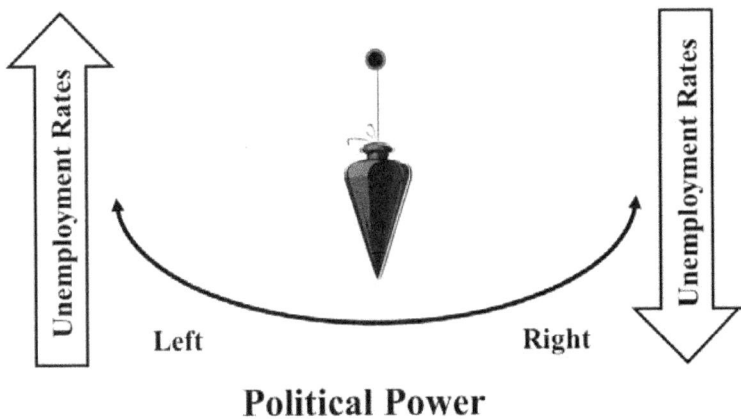

Figure 9. The Effect of Political Party on Unemployment Rates

Old Gadfly: Yes, IM, what you are talking about are the real facts. And, what disappoints me is when people like former President Clinton try to diminish reality with comments like "congressional Republicans zero."

IM: What do you mean?

Old Gadfly: Look at what happened in 2007. Democrats took sizable majorities in both houses of Congress and the decreasing trend in unemployment rates, arguably enabled by the Bush tax cuts, reversed. The reversed trend continued until Republicans gained the majority in the House in 2010, reducing unemployment rates. Instead of demonizing Republicans, Clinton and Obama should be thanking House Republicans for reducing unemployment rates (see Figure 3 and Table 2).

IM: The facts paint a completely different picture than the one told by Clinton.

Old Gadfly: As Professor Lakoff would tell us, cognitive science research has revealed that it is the frame that matters--if facts fit, great; if not, they are irrelevant.[44]

IM: Bingo. Obama and Clinton are capitalizing on the narrative frame through plausible story-telling. Ironically, I found an interesting book on one of your bookshelves that also addresses this type of behavior in political campaigns. Anthony Downs explained this dynamic in his book, *An Economic Theory of Democracy*. According to Downs, political parties are only focused on gaining political offices. In campaigns, candidates argue that they have better ideas on promoting an ideal society. Uncertainty is critical because it allows parties to develop ideologies that exploit uncertainty. Ideologies use metaphors or verbal images of a good society and political parties (and their corresponding political candidates) argue that only their ideology is capable of constructing an ideal society. Ideologies then become weapons in political struggles.[45] As an example of an ideological weapon, the opening paragraph in Lakoff's book, *Thinking Points*, claimed, "America today is in danger. It faces the threat of domination by a radical, authoritarian right wing that refers to itself as 'conservative,' as if it were preserving and promoting American values. In fact, it has been trampling on them."[46] John Podesta, founder and former CEO and President, Center for American Progress, praised Lakoff for his intellectual heavy lifting: "Lakoff serves progressives well by explaining how language and moral framing equals power in politics. Thinking Points helps leaders and activists alike to turn this knowledge into a compelling vision for society."[47] Lakoff gave himself much of the credit for the major shift in political power in both houses of Congress in November of 2006.[48]

Old Gadfly: Interesting. How do you see this dynamic playing out in today's political campaigning?

IM: When you understand Downs' political party ideology theory, its manifestation becomes very obvious. For example, I see this dynamic

---

[44] George Lakoff, *Thinking Points: Communicating Our American Values and Vision*, (New York, NY: Farrar, Straus and Giroux, 2006), p. 14. The contents of this book are available at http://www.cognitivepolicyworks.com/wordpress/wp-content/uploads/Thinking-Points-BETA1.pdf.

[45] Anthony Downs, *An Economic Theory of Democracy*, (New York, NY: Harper Collins Publishers, 1957), p. 96.

[46] Lakoff, *Thinking Points*, p. xi.

[47] Podesta's statement of affirmation is on the back cover of *Thinking Points*.

[48] Jeffrey Feldman, *Framing the Debate: Famous Presidential Speeches and How Progressives Can Use Them to Change the Conversation*, (with an introduction by George Lakoff; Brooklyn, NY: Ig Publishing, 2007), pp. xi-xii.

playing out in two major ways. First, why would Clinton speak at the DNC? Clinton was not on speaking terms with Obama for months after Obama's tactics against his wife, Hillary, during the Democrat presidential primary in 2008. According to Edward Klein, in his book, *The Amateur*, Clinton believes Obama is utterly "incompetent" and has caused great damage to our nation.[49] So, the only way to explain Clinton's behavior is with Downs's observation that political parties are focused on political power. Second, while Clinton may despise Obama for incompetence, they both embrace the same verbal image of an ideal society. The Democrat verbal image of an ideal society reflects the vision of collective liberty, guaranteed by a strong central government to ensure "shared responsibility" and "shared prosperity" as the American dream. Of course, to achieve this dream requires egalitarian policies.

Old Gadfly: What do you mean by egalitarian?

IM: Egalitarianism is a belief that it is morally expected to ensure equality of outcome for all, even if this requires restricting freedoms for some. Obamacare's individual mandate is a clear example of an egalitarian policy. In this case, there is no freedom to choose. If an individual chooses not to be insured, then he or she will pay a penalty in the form of tax to the Internal Revenue Service. And, despite the top 1% of our tax filers already paying more than 38.7% of federal tax revenues (as of 2009) while nearly 50% are paying none of it, the 1% are demonized for not paying their fair share.[50] Using data collected by the Congressional Budget Office, the following graph (Figure 10) shows how the top 1% compares with the lower 40% (fourth and fifth quintiles).[51]

Since 1991, the top 1% has been progressively paying more, while the bottom 40% are not only not paying any at all, but receiving more in the form of tax credits (payments from the federal government). This graph is evidence of a very progressive tax system. Yet, Democrats want to impose an even greater tax burden on the top 1%. Egalitarianism, especially in the form of taxation, is the progressive movement's key mechanism for promoting social justice.

---

[49] Edward Klein, *The Amateur*, (Washington, D.C.: Regnery Publishing, Inc., 2012), pp. 5-12.

[50] Chris Conover, "Flight of the Millionaires: Reasons to Give Thanks for the One Percent," *Forbes.com*, July 23, 2012. Retrieved from http://www.forbes.com/sites/chrisconover/2012/07/23/flight-of-millionaires-reasons-to-give-thanks-for-one-percent-taxes/

[51] "The Distribution of Household Income and Federal Taxes, 2008 and 2009," Congressional Budget Office, July 10, 2012, available at http://www.cbo.gov/publication/ 43373

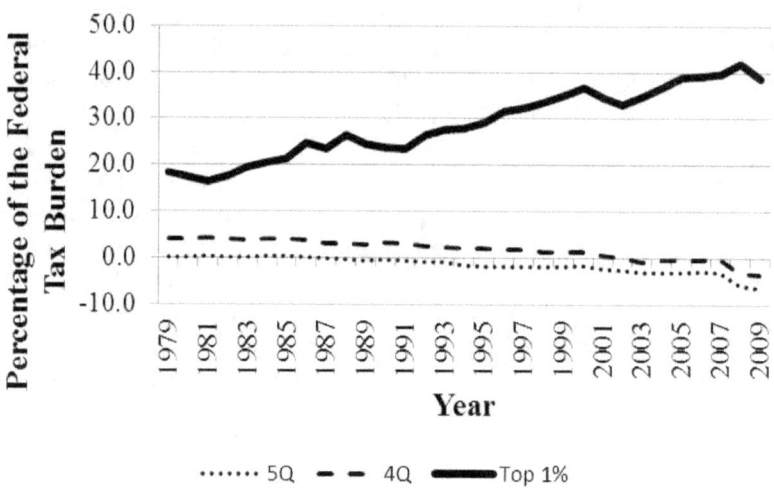

Figure 10. A Comparison of the Federal Tax Burden between the Top 1% and the Bottom 40% (Fifth [5Q] and Fourth [4Q] Quintiles) between 1979 and 2009.

Old Gadfly: Hmmm. Progressive. I have heard people use this term before. Progressive means wanting progress does it not?

IM: The meaning is far more complex than simply wanting progress. Progressivism is an entire philosophy that derives its inspiration from European socialism and statist administrative practices. Hayek, in his *The Road to Serfdom,* provided a powerful analysis of progressivism in Germany and the Soviet Union. Hayek devoted an entire chapter to the role political correctness plays in promoting progressive values while "punishing" those who do not embrace them. This chapter was entitled, "The End of Truth." Labels such as extremist, racist, homophobe, xenophobe, and others tend to be spouted by progressives on the left end of the political spectrum. Bill Lind provided an interesting and sobering explanation on the origins of political correctness at the web site, *Accuracy in Academia.*[52] According to Lind, political correctness is cultural Marxism. Lind also claimed political correctness (PC) resulted in tens of millions of deaths around the world. He called it "the disease of ideology."[53] This disease is what C. S. Lewis warned about in *The Abolition of Man*--how

---

[52] Bill Lind, "The Origins of Political Correctness," *Accuracy in Media,* February 5, 2000. Retrieved from http://www.academia.org/the-origins-of-political-correctness/

[53] Ibid.

"conditioners condition the conditioned."[54]   Lewis wrote this book in reaction to society-wide experiments by Lenin, Stalin, and Hitler in the mid-1940s.   Ronald Pestritto provides an even more modern and compelling analysis of the progressive movement in his book, *Woodrow Wilson and the Roots of Modern Liberalism.*[55] In today's public narrative, progressivism means "moving forward."

Old Gadfly: Wait a minute. "Moving forward."   That's the Obama campaign slogan: "forward."

IM: This is no coincidence, Gadfly. The attacks on the wealthy in defense of the middle class is the same class warfare promoted by Karl Marx in alleging bourgeoisie (those who controlled centers of production) exploitation of the proletariat (labor force).

Old Gadfly: Are you suggesting that Obama and those who endorse him are socialists?

IM: I am amazed at how reluctant people are to acknowledge this likelihood. Perhaps this is so because of political correctness. Yet, here is how socialism is defined:

> A theory or system of social organization that advocates the vesting of the ownership and control of the means of production and distribution, of capital, land, etc., in the community as a whole. . . . (in Marxist theory) the stage following capitalism in the transition of a society to communism, characterized by the imperfect implementation of collectivist principles.[56]

Old Gadfly: If I understand the definition correctly, capitalism is presumed to inevitably fail, which is where socialism becomes merely a transitional phase between capitalism and communism. Socialism cannot be a permanent state because it cannot achieve satisfactory collectivist principles. Thus, communism, with its political elite centrally managing affairs to achieve equality for the masses, becomes the inevitable means for perfect implementation of collectivist principles. Professor Lakoff clearly supports this theory when he makes claims that any wealth created in America belongs to the commonwealth--all the people.[57] So far, we seem

---

[54] C. S. Lewis, *The Abolition of Man*, (New York, NY: Simon & Schuster, 1944).

[55] Ronald J. Pestritto, *Woodrow Wilson and the Roots of Modern Liberalism*, (New York, NY: Rowman & Littlefield Publishers, Inc., 2005).

[56] "Socialism," *Dictionary.com Unabridged.* Retrieved from http://dictionary.reference.com/ browse/socialism

[57] Lakoff, *Whose Freedom? Op cit.*, pp. 155-156.

to be describing our understanding of the progressive Democrat vision for America. How about the conservative Republican vision?

IM: The Republican vision has great faith in the goodness and innovativeness of American citizens to live virtuously within their communities while exercising liberty in the pursuit of happiness. Of course, these are two of the three unalienable rights endowed by the Creator. Life, the third unalienable right, seems to be a right that has been amended by human beings. In politically correct terms, life is now subordinated to reproductive rights. Now, this is a complex issue, Gadfly, and I want us to discuss it in a near future conversation because I think this issue, more than any other, tests our ability as a civilized nation to truly live virtuously in a truly just society.

Old Gadfly: I look forward to the conversation about reproductive rights.

IM: Meanwhile, the following models graphically depict the Democrat and Republican visions of America.

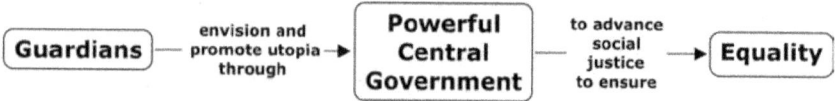

Figure 11. The Progressive Democrat Vision for America

Gadfly, progressives have a fundamental belief that the majority within society lack the intellectual capacity to understand, let alone make decisions about, complex social, political, and economic matters in the modern world. Charles Lindblom argued this position in his book, *Inquiry and Change.*[58] Therefore, political elite, in the form of guardians are needed.[59] Conservative Republicans, on the other hand, have a different vision, as depicted in the following model.

---

[58] Charles Lindblom, *Inquiry and Change: The Troubled Attempt to Understand & Shape Society,* (New Haven, CT: Yale University Press, 1990), pp. 27-29. Lindblom also argued about the limitations of the political elite to solve societal issues in "The Science of Muddling through," *Public Administration Review,* Volume 19, Number 2 (1959), pp. 79-88. In a rebuttal to Lindblom's thesis, Ronald J. Scott, Jr. argued that much more can be accomplished in the modern world in "The Science of Muddling through Revisited," *Emergence: Complexity and Organization,* Volume 12, Number 1 (2012), pp. 5-18.

[59] For arguments against the justification and logic for guardians in a democracy, see Robert Dahl, *On Democracy,* (New Haven, CT: Yale University Press, 1998), pp. 69-80.

Figure 12. The Conservative Republican Vision for America

As you can see from this vision, Gadfly, conservative Republicans seek prosperity and peace as outcomes as opposed to equality. Conservative Republicans believe people are created equal by their Creator, with the capacity to be creative and productive. F. A. Hayek explains this view in a 1945 article, "The Use of Knowledge in Society."[60] Hayek claimed that it is the individual, through his or her right to life and liberty, that envisions the ideas necessary for the pursuit of happiness; and, that true innovation occurs at the individual level and within the communities within which he or she lives, works, and plays.

Progressive Democrats, on the other hand, believe governments are necessary to take from some individuals to give to others through policies inspired by social justice. Their power in pursuing such policies is completely dependent upon establishing and sustaining perceived oppressed classes of people, such as the poor, the middle class, immigrants, gays, and so forth. In the process, these groups are coopted into indentured classes.

Old Gadfly: This is all fascinating and sobering, IM, which brings us back to the topic for today's conversation: President Clinton's role in the good economy of the 1990s. What does your analysis reveal about this period?

IM: First of all, most of us, including Ivy League and London School economists, underestimated the role President Reagan and the states played in enabling the economic conditions that led to economic growth in the 90s. Two of Reagan's major actions included (a) promoting deregulation of the airline industry, which was critical to operating in a globalized economy; and (b) taking a leadership role in bringing the Cold War to an end. I don't think we have time to discuss the Cold War victory in this conversation. But, I believe it significantly contributed to certainty

---

[60] F. A. Hayek, "The Use of Knowledge in Society," *The American Economic Review,* Vol. 35, No. 4 (September 1945), pp. 519-530.

and confidence in support of a growing economy and greater prosperity.

Old Gadfly: Tell me more about deregulating the airline industry.

IM: Most of us forget that it was President Carter who signed into law the Airline Deregulation Act of 1978. Yet, it was President Reagan who championed its enactment, along with his major tax reform (which removed "over 3 million low income people from the tax rolls").[61] Airline deregulation brought down prices to the consumer[62] and made U.S. companies more adaptive and profitable[63] in the international system.

Old Gadfly: I seem to recall that states, not the federal government, played a role in deregulating banks.

IM: When we hear politicians talk about deregulation of the financial sector, we seem to understand this to mean Presidential fiscal policy. For the financial sector during the 70s through the 90s, state legislators played a major role in deregulating banking practices. In their article, "Big Bad Banks? The Winners and Losers from Bank Deregulation in the United States," Thorsten Beck, Ross Levine, and Alexey Levkov concluded from their analyses that state-level bank deregulation had two major effects.[64] The first effect was intensified competition and improved performance. The second effect tightened income distribution where incomes increased below the median national income level. This state-led banking deregulation accounted for a lot of the economic growth during the 1990s. Clinton had nothing to do with this dynamic.

Old Gadfly: What you are telling me is that federalism works, especially when respecting the respective roles public and private sectors play in the economy at all levels of government.

IM: Absolutely. But it is far more complicated when trying to understand what is called the "New Financial Architecture" (NFA) at the federal level. James Crotty compellingly explained the structural flaws in

---

[61] Clyde H. Farnsworth, "Washington Talk: The Bureaucracy; Promise of Deregulation Proved Tough to Keep," *The New York Times*, August 18, 1988. Retrieved from http://www.nytimes.com/1988/08/18/us/washington-talk-the-bureaucracy-promise-of-deregulation-proved-tough-to-keep.html?pagewanted=all&src=pm

[62] John M. Cost, "Effects of Airline Deregulation," Mackinac Center for Public Policy, October 1, 1988. Retrieved from http://www.mackinac.org/6358

[63] Fred L. Smith, Jr. and Braden Cox, "Airline Deregulation," Library of Economics and Liberty. Retrieved from http://www.econlib.org/library/Enc/AirlineDeregulation.html

[64] Thorsten Beck, Ross Levine, and Alexey Levkov, "Big Bad Banks? The Winners and Losers from Bank Deregulation in the United States," *The Journal of Finance*, Volume 65, Issue 5 (October 2010), pp. 1637-1667.

the NFA system in his article, "Structural Causes of the Global Financial Crisis: A Critical Assessment of the 'New Financial Architecture.'"[65] Crotty concluded from his analysis that the lightly regulated NFA, in combination with the propensity for government bailouts, allowed and essentially encouraged financial institutions to take far greater risk to enhance profits and bonuses. The dilemma in this dynamic was to either increase regulation or avoid bailouts. Crotty concluded that lighter regulation promotes innovation. Thus, while not suggested by Crotty, it seems that government bailouts should not be allowed in order to reduce the incentives for excessive risk.

Old Gadfly: Why are decision-makers in the federal government so inclined to provide bailouts?

IM: I suspect this inclination is tied to crony capitalism.

Old Gadfly: What do you mean by crony capitalism?

IM: Politicians and executives from large financial firms and businesses make strange bedfellows. Crony capitalism is not tied to either political party. In 1998, Senator Joe Lieberman published a powerful article on this phenomenon, especially as it relates to campaign contributions.[66] Lieberman said this form of corruption is a serious threat against experiments in self-government. This is why, when asked what kind of government our Founders had formed, Benjamin Franklin replied, "A republic, if we can keep it." Lieberman emphasized that Franklin was concerned that when there is collaboration of greed with political power, there is a tendency toward monarchy.

Old Gadfly: Is there any evidence of this kind of collaboration?

IM: After reading Lieberman's article, I did a little more research. In the 2008 Presidential campaign, both candidates--McCain and Obama-- pledged to use only public funds for their campaigns. By the third Presidential debate on October 15, McCain confronted Obama about violating this pledge.[67] Obama never responded to McCain's challenge; also conspicuously absent was no probing for a response by the debate moderator, Bob Schieffer of *CBS News*. When the election was over, the

---

[65] James Crotty, "Structural Causes of the Global Financial Crisis: A Critical Assessment of the 'New Financial Architecture," Cambridge Journal of Economics, Volume 33, Issue 4 (2009), pp. 563-580.

[66] Joseph Lieberman, "A Republic – If We Can Keep It," *The Atlantic Monthly*, (July 1998), Vol. 282, No. 1, pp. 14-17. Available at http://www.theatlantic.com/issues/98jul/republic.htm

[67] See the transcript for this debate archived at the Commission on Public Debates at http://www.debates.org/ index.php? page=october-15-2008-debate-transcript

Federal Elections Commission reported that Obama spent $730 million on his campaign compared to McCain's $333 million.[68]

Old Gadfly: Is it coincidental that Jeffery Immelt, Chairman and CEO of General Electric, is Obama's Jobs Council Chairman? General Electric had significant equity in *NBC News*. It did not go unnoticed that *NBC News* did not cover the fact that despite billions in profits, GE paid no federal taxes.[69] Then there is Robert Rubin, who after 26 years with Goldman Sachs, served eight years as President Clinton's Secretary of the Treasury. Then he joined Citigroup where during his tenure he received $126 million in cash and stock.[70]

IM: Let me add to what you just described with another quick example of crony capitalism. President Obama recruited Timothy Geithner for his Secretary of the Treasury. Prior to this position, Geithner served for 10 years as the President of the Federal Reserve Bank of New York. Most of the major institutions receiving government bailouts stemming from the 2008 financial crisis operated within his jurisdiction. Of all the crony capitalism, the political corruption associated with Wall Street firms is almost beyond comprehension. During the peak of the financial crisis, Geithner's Federal Reserve Bank told AIG (American International Group, Inc.) to limit regulated disclosures.[71] I also was shocked to see the major extent of *New York Times* reporting on these matters; yet, there has been no traction in Washington to move financial affairs in a constructive direction.[72] And, by constructive direction, I do not mean more regulation. I do mean a common sense approach that allows financial firms to legally contribute to wealth creation with the freedom to innovate and to take risk,

[68] Data collected from Open Secrets.org, available at http://www.opensecrets.org/pres08/index.php

[69] Paul Farhi, "On NBC, the Missing Story about Parent Company General Electric," The Washington Post, March 29, 2011. Retrieved from http://articles.washingtonpost.com/2011-03-29/lifestyle/35261356_1_nbc-news-lauren-kapp-news-with-brian-williams

[70] Eric Dash and Louise Story, "Rubin Leaving Citigroup; Smith Barney for Sale," *The New York Times*, January 9, 2009. Retrieved from http://www.nytimes.com/2009/01/10/business/10rubin.html?_r=2&hp&

[71] Hugh Son, "Geithner's Fed Told AIG to Limit Swaps Disclosure (Update 3)," *Bloomberg.com*, January 7, 2010. Retrieved from http://www.bloomberg.com/apps/news?pid=newsarchive& sid= aXIvW4igKV38

[72] "Federal Reserve Bank of New York," *The New York Times*. Retrieved from http://topics.nytimes.com/top/reference/timestopics/organizations/f/federal_reserve_bank_of_new_york/index.html

while letting the shareholders, not the American taxpayer, enable or constrain the amount of risk they are willing to accept.

Old Gadfly: Excellent analysis, IM.

We do not have time in today's conversation to discuss Hannah Arendt's observations in her book *The Origins of Totalitarianism*. But, let me just plant a seed for a future conversation, because it is related to the dynamics we are now discussing. Arendt dedicated a chapter to crony capitalism. It is entitled, "The Political Emancipation of the Bourgeoisie."[73] The implications of what we are currently witnessing clearly follow the pattern described by Arendt.

Let's get back to today's topic. Were there any monetary policies that aggravated the financial crisis?

IM: Yes. John Taylor, a noted economist, conducted analysis[74] of the financial crisis and asserted the following:

> What caused the financial crisis? What prolonged it? Why did it worsen so dramatically more than a year after it began? Rarely in economics is there a single answer to such questions, but the empirical research . . . strongly suggests that specific government actions and interventions should be first on the list of answers to all three.[75]

Taylor's analysis provided empirical evidence that monetary policy (i.e., deliberately suppressing interest rates based on fear of deflation as experienced in Japan) contributed to excesses in the housing market, which significantly amplified the boom and bust cycle, resulting in the financial crisis.[76] He further explained that the crisis was global in scope, where the U.S. Federal Reserve monetary policy (i.e., interest rates unusually low) likely influenced similar policy throughout the international system.[77] According to Taylor, the unusual reduction in federal rates (from 5.25% to 2%) also had a noticeable effect on oil prices, which jumped from $70 to

---

[73] Hannah Arendt, *The Origins of Totalitarianism*, (New York, NY: Schocken Books, 2004 [originally published 1948]).

[74] John B. Taylor, *The Financial Crisis and the Policy Responses: An Empirical Analysis of What Went Wrong*. Working Paper 14631, January 2009. National Bureau of Economic Research, Cambridge, MA. Copyright 2009 by John B. Taylor. Retrieved from http://www.nber.org/papers/w14631.pdf

[75] Ibid, p. 1. Permission to quote the text granted by John B. Taylor.

[76] Ibid, p. 4.

[77] Ibid, p. 9.

$140 per barrel between August 2007 and July 2008.[78]

Taylor did not address Quantitative Easing (or QE) monetary policy (printing new money) and the global implications such as the so called "Arab Spring." Grain, which is needed for such food items as bread, is a commodity. Food prices spiked by 37% in the 2007 to 2008 timeframe.[79] While Federal Reserve Chairman Bernanke played down the effect of QE on commodity prices,[80] others disagree, claiming that there is such a relationship.[81]

Old Gadfly: Not a pretty picture in terms of monetary policy. But let's get back to the National Financial Architecture. Were there any fiscal policies that aggravated flaws in the system?

IM: Yes. But when I ask people about it, hardly anyone is aware of any of the particulars. For example, in 2011, Gretchen Morgenson and Joshua Rosner revealed the causes and conditions for the global financial crisis in their book, *Reckless Endangerment: How Outsized Ambition, Greed, and Corruption Led to Economic Armageddon.*[82] The key trigger that moved our nation to the financial crisis was the Federal Housing Enterprises Financial Safety and Soundness Act of 1992.[83] The law was essentially written by James Johnson, Chief Executive Officer of Fannie Mae, in cooperation with a Democrat-controlled Congress. Johnson also recruited activists from ACORN to pressure mortgage lenders into making risking loans, that

---

[78] Ibid, p. 20.

[79] Rami Zurayk, Use Your Loaf: Why Food Prices Were Crucial in the Arab Spring. *The Guardian,* July 16, 2011. Retrieved from http://www.guardian.co.uk/lifeandstyle/2011/jul/17/bread-food-arab-spring

[80] Ben Bernanke on Crude Oil and How QE May Have Fed Commodity Prices. *CommodityOnline.com,* July 11, 2013. Retrieved from http://www.commodityonline.com/news/ben-bernanke-on-crude-oil-and-how-qe-may-have-fed-commodity-prices-55377-3-55378.html

[81] John Kemp, Quantitative Easing and Commodity Markets. Commodities-Now.com, November 1, 2010. Retrieved from http://www.commodities-now.com/news/general/3972-quantitative-easing-and-commodity-markets.html

[82] Gretchen Morgenson and Joshua Rosner, *Reckless Endangerment: How Outsized Ambition, Greed, and Corruption Led to Economic Armageddon,* (New York, NY: Henry Holt and Company, 2011).

[83] The Federal Housing Enterprises Financial Safety and Soundness Act of 1992 is the short title for Title XIII, Government Sponsored Enterprises (i.e., Fannie Mae and Freddie Mac), which is part of a larger Public Law Number 102-550, The Housing and Community Development Act of 1992, approved by President George H. W. Bush on October 28, 1992. Details of the text and Congressional action are available at http://thomas.loc. gov/cgi-bin/bdquery/z?d102:h.r.05334:

is, sub-prime mortgages to low income, high risk applicants. According to Morgenson and Rosner, ACORN (Association of Community Organizations for Reform Now) executives were initially reluctant to take part in the scheme until Johnson provided "hundreds of thousands of dollars" in grants.[84] In 1994, President Clinton launched the National Partners in Homeownership. This initiative was a private-public effort to significantly increase the numbers of homeowners.[85]

As a matter of fiscal policy, many people blame the financial crisis on deregulation, such as in the Financial Services Modernization Act of 1999. This Act eliminated a provision of Glass-Steagall that had established legal barriers between financial investment and banking institutions. Yet, there is no evidence that the removal of this provision led to any fraudulent activities. While three Republicans--Phil Gramm, Jim Leach, and Thomas Bliley--are implicated for their role, the vast majority of the politicians who worked with the financial sector in advancing corrupted practices were Democrat. For example, Congressman Barney Frank and Senator Chris Dodd played prominently in the analysis by Morgenson and Rosner. The Morgenson and Rosner book is rich with detailed patterns of corrupted activities. The evidence in *Reckless Endangerment* clearly supports the dynamics described in Crotty's article about structural causes of the financial crisis. Yet, Democrats have been roundly and immorally successful in blaming Bush policies for the economic crisis. And, what I find particularly criminal about this mess is that those hurt the most were low income minorities who were pushed into risky mortgages.[86]

Old Gadfly: IM, I am amazed that there is so much credible analysis on this topic. Did Congress commission any studies on the crisis?

IM: Yes. Congress established The National Commission on the Causes of the Financial and Economic Crisis in the United States as part of the Fraud Enforcement and Recovery Act.[87]

Old Gadfly: Well, that sounds encouraging. Did the Commission complete its task?

---

[84] Morgenson and Rosner, p. 22.

[85] Ibid, p. 1.

[86] Jacob S. Rugh and Douglas S. Massey, "Racial Segregation and the American Foreclosure Crisis," *American Sociological Review*, Volume 75, Issue 5 (October 2010), pp. 629-651.

[87] The Commission was one of the actions mandated by The Fraud Enforcement and Recovery Act, Public Law 111-21, signed into law on May 20, 2009 by President Obama. The text of the law is available at http://www. gpo. gov/fdsys/pkg/PLAW-111publ21/pdf/PLAW-111publ21.pdf

IM: Sort of. The Commission's final report in January of 2011 was listed on the *New York Times* and *Washington Post* best seller list.[88] The commission consisted of 10 commissioners, six appointed by Senator Reid and Congresswoman Pelosi and four appointed by Senator McConnell and Congressman Boehner. When the report was publicly released, only six of the 10 commissioners endorsed the report; they were the Reid and Pelosi appointees. The four commissioners appointed by McConnell and Boehner dissented from the report and were allowed a short rebuttal at the end of the report, which pointed to other potential causes not considered by the Commission. The official report placed all the blame on the financial sector with absolutely no consideration of government fiscal or monetary policy causes. Nowhere in the entire report, which is include many specific names, is Fannie Mae's James Johnson mentioned.

Old Gadfly: Am I misreading the public narrative that appears to claim the recent Bush Administration did little to stem conditions that led to the financial crisis?

IM: No. The public narrative and corresponding public sentiment, which I believe was intentionally engineered (a topic for another conversation), made Bush look incompetent.

Old Gadfly: I infer from your comment that this is not true.

IM: As early as 2003, the Bush Administration wanted stronger oversight on Fannie Mae and Freddie Mac.[89] Two years later, Republicans in the 109th Congress also pushed legislation for greater oversight in Senate Bill 190. The bill never made it out of the 20-member committee. The bill needed 12 votes in favor to defeat a filibuster. Eleven Republicans voted in favor and nine Democrats opposed.[90] So you see, efforts were under way to avoid or minimize the effects of the tidal wave by Republicans; but these efforts were thwarted by Democrats and not widely known among the voting public. Also, don't forget the public outrage about Enron and WorldCom. Bush "inherited" these "problems" and pushed for regulatory reform that became Sarbanes-Oxley.

---

[88] Financial Crisis Inquiry Commission, *The Financial Crisis Inquiry Report: Final Report of the National Commission on the Causes of the Financial and Economic Crisis in the United States*, (New York, NY: Public Affairs, 2011)

[89] Stephen Labaton, "New Agency Proposed to Oversee Freddie Mac and Fannie Mae," *The New York Times*, September 11, 2003. Retrieved from http://www.nytimes.com/2003/09/11/business/new-agency-proposed-to-oversee-freddie-mac-and-fannie-mae.html

[90] Randall Parker, "Senate Bill S. 190 in the 109th Congress and You," *Randall Parker's Completely Serious/Sometimes Funny/Bash-Free Macroeconomics Blog*, October 24, 2008. Retrieved from http://randallparker.blogspot.com/2008/10/fannie-freddie-regulations-cox.html

Old Gadfly: But, how would you account for the willingness of Congresswoman Pelosi, as the Speaker of the House, to level such harsh criticisms against Bush?[91] For example, here is just a sampling of some direct quotes:

> "The emperor has no clothes. When are people going to face the reality? Pull this curtain back"[92]

> "The situation in Iraq and the reckless economic policies in the United States speak to one issue for me, and that is the incompetence of our leader."[93]

IM: It was all rhetoric--it reinforced a narrative frame. By creating an "image" that Bush was incompetent to advance an ideal society, Democrats, especially the progressives driving their agenda, created a political bogey man for any Democrat to run against in 2006 and 2008 elections. The strategy, despite its fraudulent justification, worked. Democrats took large majorities in both houses of Congress in 2006 and that momentum helped Obama win in 2008. Don't forget the ruthlessness of the progressive politicians. Obama changed his mind about campaigning with federal funding while McCain kept to his pledge to do so, which explains why Obama spent over $760 million or $10.94 per vote versus McCain's $358 million or $5.97 per vote.[94] If we're willing to be objective about what is happening, then we cannot deny that there are too many examples of progressive politicians who are willing to say or do anything to get elected. Fred Barnes of *The Weekly Standard* warned about this in his evidence-based article, "The Colorado Model."[95]

Old Gadfly: Your analysis provides strong support for Anthony Downs's observation you described earlier in the conversation. So, before

---

[91] "Pelosi Questions Bush's Competence," *CNN.com*, May 21, 2004. Retrieved from http://www.cnn.com/ 2004/ALLPOLITICS/05/20/pelosi.bush/

[92] Ibid.

[93] Ibid.

[94] "2008 Presidential Campaign Finance" Federal Election Commission. Retrieved from http://www.fec.gov/ disclosurep/pnational.do;jsessionid=3DC9492C30B5B1DC37E12AC133C91708.w orker1

[95] Fred Barnes, "The Colorado Model: The Democrats' Plan for Turning Red States Blue," *The Weekly Standard*, Vol. 13, No. 42 (July 21, 2008). Retrieved from http://www.weeklystandard.com/Content/Public/ Articles/000/000/015/316nfdzw.asp

we stop for a glass of wine, what are our key take away points from today's conversation?

IM: I think there are four conclusions: First, Clinton's DNC lecture reinforced his "Slick Willie" legacy. Second, while he boldly took credit for a growing economic wave in the 1990s, Clinton deserves little credit for actually generating the conditions for the economic wave he merely surfed; yet, he takes no ownership for contributing to conditions that resulted in the recession he handed off to Bush. Third, Democrats, more so than Republicans, use ideology (i.e., egalitarian-based, social justice policy to promote equality in outcomes) to attain political office. Fourth, our "free press" has done a very poor job of being the watchdog of current affairs in our society. Most of what I learned about the American economy and the global financial crisis I had to glean from deep research of credible research sources. The information I found provided important insights that should guide future actions to put our economy on a healthy footing.

Old Gadfly: Thank you, IM, for your powerful analysis and reflections.

IM: For our next conversation, perhaps we can discuss the dream I had after President Obama's DNC speech. Two features of the dream frightened me: it was in black and white, and Obama had dried, parched lips.

Old Gadfly: I can't wait to hear about it.

6 AN EMPTY CHAIR

September 14, 2012
Serrano's Coffee, Monument, Colorado

IM: Gadfly, telling you about my dream following the Democratic National Convention must wait.

Old Gadfly: Why?

IM: I am heart-broken for the families of the four Americans killed in Libya; but also furious that it even happened.

Old Gadfly: Why furious?

IM: It was just last week that Clint Eastwood was sneeringly ridiculed[96] for his empty chair routine at the Republican National Convention.[97] Clint saw something in President Obama's performance, and did not need a script or teleprompter to explain it. The chair *has* been empty. Apparently, the current incumbent has had little time for the

---

[96] The liberal media demonstrated a "feeding frenzy" (another apropos idiom) in critiquing Eastwood. There were many media articles on the speech, none even close to neutral in tone. A Google search with key words, Eastwood and chair, will produce over five million returns.

[97] Clint Eastwood's Republican National Convention presentation is available at http://www.youtube.com/ watch? v= yoqKdWY692k

traditional daily intelligence briefings.[98]

Old Gadfly: How does "not taking daily intelligence briefings" implicate the President?

IM: Protecting our nation and American citizens was not his first priority. Obama's first priority was campaigning for reelection. This is obvious by his actions. He was content to seek refuge when his disciples in the media circled wagons around him claiming, "Politics stop at the water's edge."[99]

Old Gadfly: Why did they say that?

IM: Romney criticized the Administration for a State Department statement released by the American embassy in Cairo that pandered to an agitated Muslim faction. Immediately, Romney was attacked by pundits and politicians for *politicizing* a foreign policy situation. Yet, if the President happens to be a Republican, such as Reagan or Bush, the *water's edge* maxim does not apply. There is plenty of evidence to support this hypocrisy. A simple Google search produces millions of returns.[100]

Where was the same level of consideration for the maxim "politics stop at the water's edge" when Bush was dealing with serious foreign policy issues? After being armed with a **bipartisan** Joint Resolution of Congress to use military force in Iraq, Bush acted to remove a tyrant who was far more brutal than Libya's Gaddafi. Saddam Hussein was eventually captured, arrested (not assassinated by Navy SEALs), and tried in a court of law consisting of his citizen-peers.[101] Incidentally, the threat of alleged

---

[98] Marc A. Thiessen, "Why Is Obama Skipping More than Half of His Daily Intelligence Meetings?" *The Washington Post*, September 10, 2012. Retrieved from http://www.washingtonpost.com/opinions/why-is-obama-skipping-more-than-half-of-his-daily-intelligence-meetings/2012/09/10/6624afe8-fb49-11e1-b153-218509a954e1_story.html

[99] Secretary of State Hillary Clinton declared such a maxim in *Politico*, November 3, 2010. For an incredibly biased and inaccurate opinion piece, see Fred Kaplan, "Kaplan: Lessons from Libya," *The Denver Post*, September 13, 2012. Retrieved from http://www.denverpost.com/recommended/ci_21527791.

[100] A Google search using key words Reagan and "Iran-Contra" produces 1,420,000 returns. A Google search using the key words "George W. Bush" and Iraq produces 18,100,000 returns.

[101] The Joint Resolution is known at Public Law 107-243, "Authorization for Use of Military Force against Iraq Resolution of 2002," available at http://www.gpo.gov/fdsys/pkg/PLAW-107publ243/content-detail.html. In the House, 215 Republicans and 81 Democrats voted in favor of while six Republicans and 126 Democrats (including Pelosi) voted against the legislation. In the Senate, 48 Republicans and 29 Democrats (including Reid) voted in favor of while one Republican and 22 Democrats voted against the legislation. In other words, **the**

weapons of mass destruction represented only one of 12 justifications for the use of force in the Joint Resolution.

Further, the momentum for ousting Hussein was far from a George W. Bush initiative. Here is a March 2, 2000 quote from the *Congressional Record* by Senator John Kerry:

Mr. President, I want to call to the attention of my colleagues an issue that is not being raised in the otherwise informative presidential primary campaigns. It is not a theoretical issue, nor is it an issue concerning budgetary decisions.

Rather, it is an issue which sends American pilots on combat missions almost daily. It is an issue which throughout the last decade has cost the lives of hundreds of American and thousands of soldiers and civilians of other nationalities. It is an issue which threatens the peace and security of some of our closest allies, and which, if not solved, could threaten the United States with weapons of mass destruction. It is an issue which starves and holds captive twenty-two million people in conditions of unparalleled terror of their government. It is an issue which we have failed to deal with decisively, and that failure calls into question our dedication to the freedom we prize so highly for ourselves.

The issue is the continuing rule of Saddam Hussein. Nine years after the United States led a coalition to eject Iraqi forces and liberate Kuwait, Saddam continues to brutalize his people, threaten his neighbors, and develop weapons of mass destruction--earlier versions of which he used on neighboring states, on Israel, and on his own people. The good news is that sanctions have weakened his military, and his political support base has shrunk to his immediate family. All of mountainous northern Iraq and large

---

resolution passed by a significant majority of bipartisan votes. The voting record is available at http://thomas. loc. gov/cgi-bin/bdquery/D?d107:12:./temp/~bdVEqq:@@@R|/home/LegislativeData.php?n=BSS;c=107

swathes of southern Iraq are free of his control. Nonetheless, he continues to rule the central part of the country and, as Jim Hoagland pointed out in today's *Washington Post*, Saddam is likely to outlast yet another American President.[102]

Old Gadfly: IM, you are furious.

IM: Yes, I am. Most Americans never know there was legislation enacted for regime change in Iraq during the Clinton Administration.[103] And, when I recall how Bush was roundly criticized for the "mission accomplished" banner on the aircraft carrier, I can't believe how hypocritical people can be when they are the ones to politicize beyond the water's edge. The men and women on the U.S. Navy carrier group were proud of the role they played up to that point in the conflict and believed they (i.e., this particular unit) had accomplished their mission. They were especially proud to be honored by their commander in chief. Yet, progressives could not contain themselves--they had to attack Bush for apparent bravado. It's obviously alright not to keep politics at the water's edge when you're on the left side of the political spectrum. And I wonder how many more people, American and Iraqi, that had to die because Bush had to fight a two-front war, one in Iraq and one at home.

Old Gadfly: IM, are you hyperventilating?

IM: No, I am trying hard to stop thinking about the hypocrisy, and then I remember Speaker of the House Pelosi's trip to Syria in 2007 in defiance of the President and Secretary of State.[104] Now, with the demise of Assad and thousands of fatalities, we can clearly see how much this kind of rogue diplomacy worked beyond the water's edge. How many innocent civilians have been killed so far? Thousands.[105]

---

[102] *Congressional Record—Senate*, March 2, 2000, p. S1150. Retrieved from http://www.gpo.gov/fdsys/pkg/ CREC-2000-03-02/pdf/CREC-2000-03-02-pt1-PgS1150.pdf#page=1

[103] Public Law 105-338, known as the Iraq Liberation Act of 1998, was signed into law by President Clinton on October 31, 1998. The legislation was a bipartisan effort with 360 (202 Republicans, 157 Democrats) in favor of and 38 (nine Republicans, 29 Democrats) against in the House of Representatives; the Senate provided unanimous consent. For more details on the text of the legislation, major actions, and voting see http://thomas. loc.gov/cgi-bin/bdquery/z?d105:h.r.04655:

[104] See "Pelosi Shrugs Off Bush's Criticism, Meets Assad," *NBC News.com*, April 4, 2007. Retrieved from http://www.msnbc.msn.com/id/17920536/ns/world_news-mideast_n_africa/t/pelosi-shrugs-bushs-criticism-meets-assad/

[105] Saad Abedine and Ben Brumfield, "Over 37,000 Have Died in Syria's Civil War, Opposition Group Says," *CNN.com*, November 15, 2012. Retrieved from

Old Gadfly: IM, perhaps progressive Democrats, especially Pelosi, have another maxim by which they operate—life has no relevance in politics. After all, as a publicly proclaimed Catholic, Pelosi even disregards criticism from the Pope and Bishops regarding the sanctity of life. The number of 100,000 deaths in Syria is a mere pittance compared to the 55 million babies aborted since Roe vs. Wade.[106]

IM: One last point. Is Obama the captain of our ship of state?

Old Gadfly: Of course.

IM: Was he anointed or elected?

Old Gadfly: Technically, he was elected.

IM: What amazes me is when I ask those who follow him, why they like him, their eyes seem to glaze over and they begin a meditative mantra: hope . . . change . . . forward . . . hope . . . change . . . forward. Gadfly, are you still with me?

Old Gadfly: I have to admit, IM, it is somewhat hypnotic.

IM: Let me finish my point. Whether anointed or elected, the captain of the ship is expected to be accountable. If you have not read it, then I recommend you read a *Wall Street Journal* editorial published on May 14, 1952. The title of the piece was "Hobson's Choice: Responsibility and Accountability."[107]   The story stems from a collision between the USS Wasp and USS Hornet on April 26, 1952. The USS Hornet sank, and 176 crewmembers died.[108] The editorial claimed that with responsibility comes accountability. Without accountability, there is no responsibility. Whether anointed or elected, the captain of our ship of state is responsible. The *WSJ* editorial emphasized that while accountability of well-intentioned men may seem cruel, without accountability there is an end to responsibility. As history has taught, people will lose confidence and trust in leaders who act as though they are beyond accountability. Eventually, without responsible and accountable leadership, a ship of state will disintegrate into chaos and no purpose.

---

http://www.cnn.com/2012/11/15/world/meast/syria-civil-war/index.html. More recently, see Alan Cowell, "War Deaths in Syria Said to Top 100,000. The New York Times, June 26. 2013. Retrieved from http://www.nytimes.com/2013/06/27/world/middleeast/syria.html?_r=0

[106] "Roe v. Wade: 40 Years Too May," National Right to Life Committee, January 22, 2013. Retrieved from http://www.nrlc.org/press_releases_new/Release012213.html

[107] "Hobson's Choice: Responsibility and Accountability," *The Wall Street Journal*, May 14, 1952.

[108] A short history of the USS Hobson and the incident is available at http://www.history.navy.mil/danfs/h7/ hobson.htm

Old Gadfly: But, IM, your story is 60 years old. Do you think there are relevant insights for today's current affairs?

IM: Yes. Our ship of state is confronted with dangerous conditions. During Clinton's era, between 1992 and 2000, a period within the past 20 years, there were numerous attacks on US sovereign territory and American citizens. Here are some of the most significant.

- On February 26, 1993, terrorists attacked the World Trade Center in New York, killing six people.[109]
- On June 25, 1996, 23 American airmen died and over 300 were wounded in the Khobar Towers bombing in Dhahran, Saudi Arabia.[110]
- On August 7, 1998, a series of American embassy bombings linked to the Egyptian Islamic Jihad in Dar Es Salaam, Tanzania and Nairobi, Kenya killed hundreds of people.[111]
- On October 12, 2000, the USS Cole was attacked off the coast of Yemen, killing 17 and wounding 39 sailors.[112]

And during the current President's tenure, we had the underwear bomber[113] and the Fort Hood shootings. The latter case has been held hostage to political correctness.[114]

---

[109] Richard Bernstein, "Explosion at the Twin Towers; 4 Are Convicted in Bombing at the World Trade Center that Killed 6, Stunned U.S.," *The New York Times*, March 5, 1994. Retrieved from http://www.nytimes.com/ 1994/03/05/nyregion/explosion-twin-towers-4-are-convicted-bombing-world-trade-center-that-killed-6.html?pagewanted=all&src=pm

[110] Philip Shenon, 23 U.S. Troops Dies in Truck Bombing in Saudi Base. *The New York Times*, June 26, 1996. Retrieved from http://partners.nytimes.com/library/world/africa/062696binladen.html

[111] Brian Bennett, Al Qaeda Operative Key to 1998 U.S. Embassy Bombings Killed in Somalia. *The Los Angeles Times*, June 12, 2011. Retrieved from http://articles.latimes.com/2011/jun/12/world/la-fg-embassy-bombings-20110612

[112] The USS Cole Bombing. *Famous Cases & Criminals*. The Federal Bureau of Investigation. Retrieved from http://www.fbi.gov/about-us/history/famous-cases/uss-cole

[113] Josh Meyer and Peter Nicholas, Obama Calls Jet Incident a "Serious Reminder." *The Los Angeles Times*, December 29, 2009. Retrieved from http://articles.latimes.com/print/2009/dec/29/nation/la-na-plane-terror29-2009dec29

[114] Experts Debate Whether Fort Hood Shootings Were Terrorism or "Workplace Violence." *The Houston Chronicle*, September 15, 2012. Retrieved from

Old Gadfly: What is your point, IM?

IM: As we approached the anniversary of the September 9, 2001 terrorist attacks, which, by the way, resulted in more casualties than the attack on Pearl Harbor, the captain of our ship of state should have been far more tuned in regarding threats to America.

Old Gadfly: Thus, your point about the Benghazi tragedy of September 11, 2012 with four more Americans dead as a result of terrorism. I can see why you agree with Clint Eastwood's empty chair message.

---

http://blog.chron.com/txpotomac/2012/09/experts-debate-fort-hood-shootings-terrorism-or-workplace-violence-islamist-extremism/

7 DRY, PARCHED LIPS

September 23, 2012
O'Malley's Pub & Grill, Palmer Lake, Colorado

IM: Gadfly, I apologize for taking so long in reporting my dream after President Obama accepted the Democratic National Convention nomination for president.

Old Gadfly: What happened?

IM: Quite frankly, I am recovering from an illness. My doctor has since medicated me for high blood pressure. But I must say that I took a triple dose of my medicine while watching the *60 Minutes* interview of President Obama tonight, September 23, 2012. Steve Kroft acted as though he were interviewing God, Himself, and grateful for not being turned into stone for asking even softball questions.

Old Gadfly: Your dream and the Kroft interview caused your blood pressure to rise?

IM: Yes, for what they symbolized.

Old Gadfly: In our last conversation, you said the dream was in black and white and that President Obama's white toothy smile was bounded by dry, parched lips.

IM: I'll get to the meaning of the black and white later. For now, I want to focus on the dry, parched lips.

Old Gadfly: You have my attention.

IM: I wanted to know the meaning of Obama's dry, parched lips. I thought long and hard about why this image caught my attention. Then, I remembered a book by Fyodor Dostoevsky, *The Brothers Karamazov*.

Old Gadfly: Dostoevsky? Are you referring to the author of *Crime and Punishment?*

IM: Yes.

Old Gadfly: Dostoevsky wrote in the late 1800s.

IM: You are well-read, Gadfly. What is your recollection of how to characterize Dostoevsky's Russia in the late 1800s?

Old Gadfly: As I recall, Russia was still pretty much a feudal state. Peasants were at the mercy of royalty. And Dostoevsky was imprisoned for views contrary to political elite.

IM: This is true. He even faced a firing squad for his political dissent. Later, he wrote *The Brothers Karamazov,* which was considered a biographical sketch of his family within the context of a harsh Russian culture.

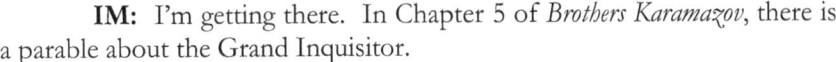

Old Gadfly: How does this relate to President Obama?

IM: I'm getting there. In Chapter 5 of *Brothers Karamazov,* there is a parable about the Grand Inquisitor.

Old Gadfly: Do you mean as in the Spanish Inquisition?

IM: Yes. As most of us know, the Spanish Inquisition took place between the 1400s and early 1800s.[115]

Old Gadfly: Are you trying to indict the Catholic Church?

IM: Absolutely not. The history and role of the Catholic Church has been terribly misrepresented and misunderstood, even within the context of the Spanish Inquisition--a story for another day. Yet, the inquisition, as reported in *The Brothers Karamazov,* is a story that must be understood within today's context.

Old Gadfly: I want to hear more.

IM: In Dostoevsky's parable, an old Spanish Cardinal observed a man healing people within a crowd. The man was Jesus Christ. The Cardinal had Him arrested and sent to the dungeons. Later in the day, the Grand Inquisitor visited Jesus, relishing the opportunity to admonish Him for not giving in to the three temptations. When face to face with Jesus, the

---

[115] For a different perspective on how the Inquisition has generally been portrayed, see Henry Kamen, *The Spanish Inquisition: A Historical Revision,* (New Haven, CT: Yale University Press, 1998). For an excellent book review, see Richard Kagan, "A Kinder, Gentler Inquisition," *The New York Times,* April 19, 1998. Retrieved from http://www.nytimes.com/books/98/04/19/reviews/980419.19kagent.html

Inquisitor went on to explain to Him all the good things he and other church administrators had done for the people. He provided example after example. Jesus stood there looking into the Inquisitors eyes with no response to any of the claims. The Grand Inquisitor then emphasized that people want the church to provide for their personal safety and security. Disappointed that Jesus offered no reaction or response, the Inquisitor said, "I have given you evidence of all the things I have done for the people; yet, you give no affirmation to what I have done for them." The Inquisitor continued, "I know your purpose for dying on the cross was to give people freedom to make choices. You had faith in their capacity to make good decisions." Jesus continued eye contact with no response. The Inquisitor further pressed Jesus: "Unlike you, I know people don't know how to make good decisions. This is why they need people like me, who know much better how they should live their lives." Exasperated, the Inquisitor finished with a confession: "I also know that people like me have aligned themselves with the devil to satisfy earthly needs and desires." At that moment, Jesus gently leaned forward, kissed the Grand Inquisitor on his dry, parched lips, and walked away.

Old Gadfly: Powerful! Who is today's Grand Inquisitor?

IM: I know what I am about to suggest is not politically correct; yet, I choose to be a man with a chest.

Old Gadfly: Excellent metaphor, IM. You are suggesting men without chests represent the consequences of political correctness as argued by C.S. Lewis's *The Abolition of Man*. Please continue your thought.

IM: President Obama is a modern Grand Inquisitor, and members of the progressive movement represent the modern secular church.

Old Gadfly: IM, the comparison seems bold and harsh at the same time. And the implications of the parable are disconcerting. How do you explain the symbolism of black and white in your dream?

IM: The black and white distinction symbolizes the past. President Obama and his collaborators want to shape America in ways similar to a previous era--an era where political elite moved entire nations in the direction of a collective utopia. Notice Obama's campaign slogan is "forward," which seems counterintuitive when understanding the progressive ideology.[116] Many intellectuals attempted to bring such thinking to the United States in the early 1930s. Amity Shlaes described

---

[116] A "forward" slogan has been tied to Marxism. See Victor Morton, "New Obama Slogan Has Long Ties to Marxism, Socialism," *The Washington Times*, April 30, 2012. Retrieved from http://www.washingtontimes. com /blog/inside-politics/2012/apr/30/new-obama-slogan-has-long-ties-marxism-socialism/

these efforts with significant evidence in Chapter 2 of *The Forgotten Man*.[117] By the way, unlike some recent comparisons to Abraham Lincoln, especially by historian Doris Kearns Goodwin,[118] Obama's worldview and political approach is much closer to Vladimir I. Lenin.[119] Both were trained as lawyers and both gained immense power as community organizers, agitating and organizing for social justice and collective, not individual, freedom. The Center for American Progress is Obama's (and the progressive movement's) epicenter for today's public narrative. What more do non-Copernican drones need for evidence that the United States of America is under ideological assault?

Since there is such an urge to declare an historical legacy on the scale of Lincoln and other great presidents, I simple conducted my own comparisons of what we know about Lincoln and Lenin and how they each compare to what little we know about Obama. The following Table summarizes my quick and simple comparative analysis.

Old Gadfly: Interesting analysis, IM. I noticed in *The Hollywood Reporter* interview with Goodwin[120] that the political elite on the left emphasize Lincoln's attempt to use compromise as a means for getting the Thirteenth Amendment ratified in the Spielberg directed movie on Lincoln. I watched the movie. Compromise in this case came from others, not Lincoln. Lincoln encouraged others to use bribes and patronage to get the votes he needed. These were clearly unethical means to achieve the desired goal. Compromise is the same mantra we hear from the political left today--they call it bipartisanship. Bipartisanship means the political right compromises, not the left. The Affordable Care Health Act (or Obamacare

---

[117] Amity Shlaes, *The Forgotten Man*. (New York, NY: Harper-Collins Publishers, 2007).

[118] Jordan Zakarin, "Doris Kearns Goodwin on 'Lincoln' and Her Conversations with Obama about the 16th President," The Hollywood Reporter, December 13, 2012. Retrieved from http://www.hollywoodreporter.com/ news/doris-kearns-goodwin-lincoln-obama-393238

[119] For a biography on Vladimir Ilyich Lenin refer to the Biograph.com website at http://www.biography.com /people/vladimir-lenin-9379007?page=1

[120] Zakarin, op cit.

as it is more commonly known) is blatant evidence--not a single Republican voted for the Act in either the House or the Senate.[121]

Table 6

Comparative Analysis of Lincoln, Lenin, and Obama

Lincoln versus Obama	
Similarities	**Differences**

• Addressed relationship between central government and state rights *but* with contrary views
• Both addressed slavery:
  − Lincoln abolished it consistent with natural law
  − Obama expanded "entitlement slavery" in the name of social justice and equality to be governed by ruling class
	• Lincoln promoted American ideals
	• Obama is changing American ideals
	• Lincoln was humble; sought greatness for America
	• Obama is arrogant; seeks his own greatness

Lenin versus Obama	
Similarities	**Differences**
• Tremendous self-confidence • Trained as lawyer *and* community organizer • Political philosophy (socialistic capitalism) • An elite ruling class defines rights • Force reform through a single vanguard party (communist/progressive) • Organize masses through labor unions • Control finance and industry through a central federal government • Shape public sentiment through propaganda (e.g., government-controlled or co-opted media; OFA)	• Historical and cultural milieu • Lenin exploited a dysfunctional society already divided by class in a feudal system • Obama amplified and exploited a class society to create a dysfunctional society

---

[121] For a record of House and Senate voting on H.R. 3590 (111th Congress), Patient Protection and Affordable Care Act, see http://www.govtrack.us/congress/bill.xpd?bill=h111-3590&tab=votes

Yet, Obama and Congressional Democrats herald the Act as an epochal achievement in the spirit of compromise and bipartisanship. Without the need for a single Republican vote, Obama and his progressive Democrat caucus engineered an outcome that pushed America closer to a socialistic system. This act is a manifestation of a desire for and power of a single vanguard party your analysis revealed. Obama even told the American people the night the Act was passed "this is what change looks like."

IM: Yes. I believe far too many of America's Copernican drones, not to mention the Nobel Peace Prize committee, want to believe Obama is messianic

Old Gadfly: Why do you think Obama wants a dysfunctional society?

IM: It worked for Lenin and his successors. Further, Obama's worldview has been ideologically shaped, especially by Frank Marshall Davis and then Saul Alinsky. In simple terms, it means that in the world there are those who have and those who have not. This "class" distinction is immoral. Davis, as a member of the Communist Party, did a masterful job instilling this indelible notion in the mind of a young Barry Obama. Saul Alinsky was essential in training the younger Obama in methods to take power away from those who have it in order to give it to those who do not have it. This is why the top 1% and Wall Street institutions are conveniently targeted as those who have. This have-have not ideology also provides the model for further dividing society in terms of social issues.

Old Gadfly: Powerful arguments, IM. I see how the "have versus have-not" ideology applies to economic matters. But social issues?

IM: Even more so for social issues. Social issues are classified in terms of "rights"—those who have them, and those who don't. For example, on the issue of abortion, progressives argue that a woman has the right to reproduce. Those who argue for the sanctity of life in the womb of the mother are, according to progressives, denying that mother the "right" to keep or kill the baby. "Unwanted" pregnancies become a convenient reason to abort a baby, despite the vast majority of pregnancies resulting from consensual sexual intercourse. A secular religion is important in justifying this kind of logic.

Old Gadfly: Your analysis is very compelling. I can see how this "have-have not" ideology also applies to other social issues such as same-sex marriage and illegal immigration.

IM: Exactly. The key to perpetuating this have versus have-not model is to control the public narrative in the news, in our educational institutions, and in Hollywood productions.

Old Gadfly: Surely, other people feel differently.

IM: Absolutely. Some of my own friends disagree with me.

Old Gadfly: This must trouble you.

IM: Yes, it does. However, I just remind myself of Hannah Arendt's discovery about wide-spread comfort with mendacity in her book, *Eichmann in Jerusalem: A Report on the Banality of Evil.*[122]

Old Gadfly: Are you serious? People actually find refuge in untruthfulness?

IM: For some, yes. Now, I don't think most people deliberately embrace mendacity. The condition may be what Benedict de Spinoza (also known as Baruch Spinoza) called "human bondage" in his 15th century book, *Ethic: Demonstrated in Geometric Order and Divided into Five Parts.*[123] Human bondage is a condition where passions or emotions trump reason. Nearly 300 years later, Leon Festinger advanced his seminal theory of cognitive dissonance.[124] The theory explains the same dynamic that Spinoza called human bondage. Human bondage has occurred throughout the history of humankind. Even the Book of Proverbs 26:11 talks about dogs returning to their vomit just as fools repeat their folly.

Old Gadfly: Very powerful, IM. You obviously believe that President Obama is a modern Grand Inquisitor, similar to the guardian concept we already discussed in "The Art of Economy Surfing" conversation. Grand Inquisitors or guardians determine how the rest of us will live our lives, which sounds familiar (e.g., Mao's China, Lenin's Soviet Union, Hitler's Germany, Mussolini's Italy, Castro's Cuba, Chavez's Venezuela, and so forth). But, what if these guardians can truly make life better for everyone? After all, my progressive friends believe this is a noble thing to do.

---

[122] Hannah Arendt, *Eichmann in Jerusalem: A Report on the Banality of Evil.* (New York, NY: Penguin Classics, 2006 [Originally published in 1963]).

[123] Benedict de Spinoza, *Ethic: Demonstrated in Geometrical Order and Divided into Five Parts.* (New York, NY: Kessinger Publishing, LLC, 2010 [Originally published in 1677]).

[124] Leon Festinger, *A Theory of Cognitive Dissonance.* (Redwood City, CA: Stanford University Press, 1962)

IM: We have recorded history to be the judge of these "noble" intentions. Collective freedom is not sustainable; and, political systems based on collective freedom devolve into totalitarianism. To avoid a similar fate, our nation needs a balance of liberal and conservative values, facilitated by character-based leaders in the public and private sectors.

Old Gadfly: Your assessment sounds like the classical liberalism that characterized America during its founding as a nation.

IM: Yes, Gadfly. But there are forces working hard to prevent a balance of values. In our next conversation I want to describe one of these powerful forces: engineering public sentiment.

Old Gadfly: Thank you, IM. I look forward to our next conversation.

8 ENGINEERING PUBLIC SENTIMENT

September 29, 2012
O'Malley's Pub & Grill, Palmer Lake, Colorado

Old Gadfly: IM, you look tired and sad.

IM: I am.   As I prepared for today's conversation I found disturbing evidence to support my hunches about how politicians and the media are deliberately engineering public sentiment.

Old Gadfly: But don't both sides do it?

IM: Yes, but not to the same degree or depth. Republicans might *vet policy ideas to* **measure public sentiment**--this is not the same as **engineering public sentiment**. However, politicians and mainstream media (80% of Americans still get 80% of their news from a left-leaning mainstream media)[125] who have aligned themselves with the progressive movement deliberately engineer public sentiment and in doing so are guilty of mendacity, complicity, and duplicity. I'll explain with plenty of public domain evidence.

Old Gadfly: We talked about mendacity in our last conversation, "Dry, Parched Lips," and how wide-spread the comfort level with untruthfulness can be. How do you define complicity and duplicity?

IM: Complicity, in this case, is a state of being an accomplice in perpetrating or tolerating mendacity. Our mainstream media has been egregiously complicit. Duplicity is deceitfulness in speech or conduct. President Obama and his strategic advisors, especially David Axelrod, have

---

[125] Douglas Mackinnon, "Mainstream Media: Public Enemy No. 1," *Investors.com*, September 27, 2012. Available at http://news.investors.com/ibd-editorials-perspective/092712-627292-mainstream-media-in-league-with-obama.htm?p=full

structured their reelection campaign based on the art of duplicity. And some in the media have played deliberate roles in support of this duplicity, such as David Corn with *Mother Jones.*

Old Gadfly: These are serious allegations, IM.

IM: Yes, and I am prepared to be criticized or persecuted for speaking out. In fact, I fully expect to be punished for any number of bogus reasons. Look how the current Justice Department has cracked down on (a) states such as Voter ID laws,[126] purging voter registration records of disqualified or ineligible people,[127] and so forth; and (b) individuals, such as Arizona's Sheriff Joe Arpaio.[128] These are clear examples of the progressive movement's attempt to shift freedoms away from individuals, in violation of the first through eight Amendments to the Constitution, and states, in violation of the ninth and tenth Amendments, toward centralized power in the federal government. By the way, one of the fathers of the American progressive movement was Woodrow Wilson.[129] It was Wilson who championed the 17th Amendment to the Constitution.[130] This Amendment, more than any other, shifted

---

[126] Leigh Ann Caldwell, "Justice Department Investigating Pa. Voter ID Law," *CBSNews.com*, July 24, 2012. Available at http://www.cbsnews.com/8301-503544_162-57478605-503544/justice-department-investigating-pa-voter-id-law/

[127] Lizette Alvarez, "Search for Illegal Voters May Violate Federal Safeguards U.S. Tells Florida," *The New York Times*, June 1, 2012. Available at http://www.nytimes.com/2012/06/02/us/justice-dept-asks-florida-to-end-voter-purge.html?_r=2&&gwh=C3ADE32EFE278599970C55233F1509BF

[128] Fernanda Santos and Charlie Savage, "Lawsuit Says Sheriff Discriminated Against Latinos," *The New York Times*, May 10, 2012. Available at http://www.nytimes.com/2012/05/11/us/ justice-department-sues-arizona-sheriff-joe-arpaio.html?_r=0&gwh=7F0B5D2247847BDAB64493B4 DC241ECB

[129] See Ronald Pestritto, "Progressivism and America's Tradition of Natural Law and Natural Rights," *Natural Law, Natural Rights and American Constitutionalism*, no date. Available at http://www.nlnrac.org/critics/ american-progressivism

[130] C. H. Hoebeke, "Democratizing the Constitution: The Failure of the Seventeenth Amendment," Center for Constitutional Studies, no date. Available at http://www.nhinet.org/hoebeke.htm

political power away from individuals and the states and placed it in the federal government. As ample evidence shows, the Obama Administration is pushing this shift in ways to fully institutionalize a central, statist-oriented government, one that finds little use for an elected Congress or Supreme Court.

Old Gadfly: Wait, just this week at the United Nations, President Obama said, "True democracy -- real freedom -- is hard work. Those in power have to resist the temptation to crack down on dissent. In hard economic times, countries may be tempted to rally the people around perceived enemies, at home and abroad, rather than focusing on the painstaking work of reform."[131]

IM: Sounds great doesn't it. There are three key phrases in Obama's speech: "resist the temptation to crack down on dissent," "countries may be tempted to rally the people around perceived enemies," and "focusing on the painstaking work of reform." All three phrases clearly demonstrate duplicity. For example, as I just described, Obama and his aides *do punish dissent.*

Old Gadfly: Good point. What are your concerns about Obama's phrase, "countries may be tempted to rally the people around perceived enemies"?

IM: This phrase is the ultimate example of Obama's mendacity and duplicity. He portrays the top 1% of taxpayers as the enemy of the middle class because they do not pay their fair share. This group already pays 40% of the tax burden, while over 50% of the population receives some form of subsidy from the revenue collected from the 50% who actually pay federal income tax.[132]

---

[131] "Obama's Speech to the United Nations General Assembly—Text," *The New York Times*, September 25, 2012. Available at http://www.nytimes.com/2012/09/26/world/obamas-speech-to-the-united-nations-general-assembly-text.html?pagewanted=all&_r=0

[132] Patrick Tyrrell, "Dependence on Government at All-Time High," *The Foundry*, February 8, 2012, The Heritage Foundation. Available at http://blog.heritage.org/2012/02/08/dependence-on-government-at-all-time-high/

Old Gadfly: Yet, Obama, his lieutenants, and a complicit mainstream media demonize Romney as a "top 1% enemy" when Romney tries to explain how difficult it may be to convince the 47%, who pay no federal income tax, that he has a better idea as to how to grow the economy and to improve the quality of life for all Americans. It does not take a rocket scientist or London School of Economics Ph.D. to understand that it's the economy, stupid--even Clinton understood this: the economy produces wealth, not the government; wealth provides tax revenue for the government.

Vice Presidential candidate Paul Ryan understands this. As an example of Ryan's very clear and "non-Copernican drone" thinking on this topic, see his excellent *Wall Street Journal* critique of Jeffrey Sachs' progressive ideas of government.[133] Ryan is a threat (and enemy) to the progressive agenda. Look at how the White House's own website (See Figure 13 below) tried to rally people against Ryan's proposed budget.[134]

Obama wants Americans to believe the federal government is giving money, an average of $150,000, to millionaires and billionaires. Ryan and fellow Republicans believe this $150,000 is earned income and better left within the private sector to further create wealth and to grow the economy. With increased profits, there is increased corporate tax revenue; and with increased jobs there is

---

[133] Paul Ryan, "America's Enduring Ideal," *The Wall Street Journal*, October 1, 2011. Available at http://online.wsj.com/article/SB10001424053111903703604576589090204327736.html

[134] See "The House Republican Budget," at http://www.whitehouse.gov/2013-republican-budget

increased individual tax revenue (See Table 4, Comparison of Benefits and Costs of Private and Public Sector Job Gains and Losses).

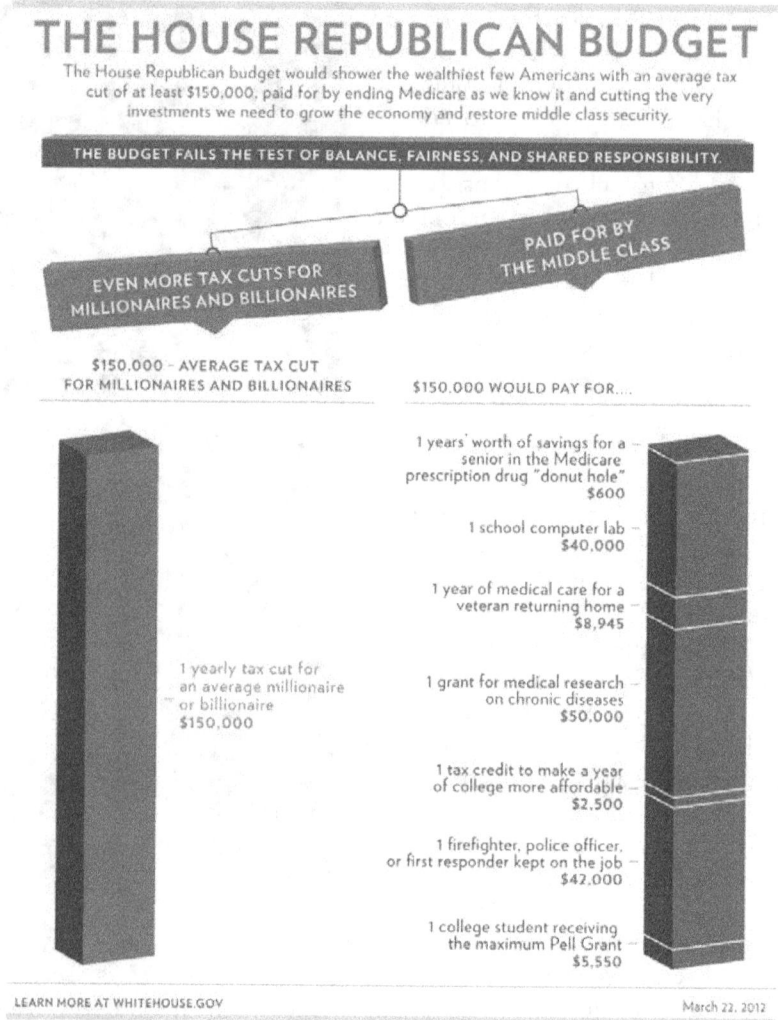

Figure 13. White House Propaganda on the House Republican Budget

IM: Yet, with a complicit Democrat-controlled Senate, there has been no budget since Obama took office. Since then, he has increased our national debt by nearly 50% in four years, thanks to annual deficit spending well in excess of a trillion dollars each year (See Figure 5, Correlation between Annual Unemployment Rates and Government Deficits between 1987 and 2011). Bush never reached an annual deficit in excess of even half a trillion, despite having to plus up a military force to defend America against a real existential threat after the Clinton Administration gutted it.

Old Gadfly: Good point, IM.

IM: You want another example? How about the Tea Party? While I am not personally affiliated with this movement, I certainly sympathize with their concerns about runaway government spending and a growing central government. This is a group, by the way, that peacefully protested without any arrests or trashing of assembly areas, unlike the Occupy Wall Street movement, which was celebrated by the Obama Administration, prominent  Democrats in Congress, and the mainstream media. Look how a complicit mainstream media has rallied people against the Tea Party (in the picture, from left to right: Kristof, Friedman, Nocera, and Dowd):

- Nicholas Kristof, of *The New York Times*, called Tea Party sympathizers "extremists," and equated Tea Party opposition to the Obama and Democratic agenda a moral equivalent to the threat from al Qaeda.[135]
- Thomas Friedman, of *The New York Times*, called the Tea Party the "Hezbollah faction" of the Republican Party.[136]

---

[135] Nicholas D. Kristof, "Republicans, Zealots and our Security," *The New York Times*, July 23, 2011. Available at
http://www.nytimes.com/2011/07/24/opinion/sunday/24kristof.html?_r=3&ref=opinion&& gwh=E4ED3DB75A30C0249A88A5E526457F07

[136] Thomas Friedman, "Can't We Do This Right?" *The New York Times*, July 26, 2011. Available at http://

- Joe Nocera, of *The New York Times*, claimed the Tea Party movement is waging jihad against America.[137]
- Maureen Dowd, a columnist for *The New York Times*, has called members of the Tea Party movement "cannibals," "zombies," and "vampires."[138]

Old Gadfly: I must say, IM, you have done your homework for our conversation. How about the reform mentioned in Obama's UN speech?

IM: The reform Obama's UN speech alluded to is part of his "hope and change" strategy. For example,

- Obama wasted no time before even being sworn in. In fact, he offered many public speeches and appearances in his self-proclaimed position: Office of the President-Elect. [139] His organization even formed a website in an attempt to seize control of the public narrative before even being sworn in.[140]
- Within a month of his inauguration, Obama spent $787 billion on a stimulus effort. This move involved no civil or bipartisan efforts, nor the normal Congressional processes for introducing and conferring on legislation. In the end, the bill passed with no Republican votes in the House and only two progressive Republican votes in the Senate (Snow and Collins from Maine).[141] As we now know, the stimulus bill, which was based

---

www.nytimes.com/2011/07/27/opinion/27friedman.html?gwh=EE92A71D5367 67F5105DF3043080245A

[137] Joe Nocera, "Tea Party's War on America," *The New York Times*, August 1, 2011. Available at http://www. nytimes.com/2011/08/02/opinion/the-tea-partys-war-on-america.html?_r=3&gwh=FAEBFE349CE64E51 422B3E6A2E1FC59F

[138] Maureen Dowd, "Washington Chain Saw Massacre," *The New York Times*, August 2, 2011. Available at http://www.nytimes.com/2011/08/03/opinion/washington-chain-saw-massacre.html?_r=3&ref=columnists& &gwh=2C7AEDD6F7E9E07CAECDCE84AD57B886

[139] For an example, see the recorded video of a policy speech at http://www.youtube.com/watch?v= XpUMHeG6aDs&playnext=1&list=PLC2316CBE6938F380&feature=results_main

[140] The website was called "change.gov." The website homepage is at http://change.gov/content/home

[141] See the details of H.R. (111th Congress), American Recovery and Reinvestment Act of 2009, at http://www.govtrack.us/congress/bills/111/hr1

on the Keynesian theory that government stimulus can generate aggregate demand, did not stimulate the economy.[142]   Other economists claim that an increase in aggregate demand **results** from a growing economy; government spending does not cause growth in the economy. Further, lofty speeches about rebuilding infrastructure and investing in green energy revealed incredible naiveté about how the broader economy and private sector businesses actually work together.[143] President John F. Kennedy understood this, which is why he is known for his axiom: "A rising tide lifts all the boats."[144]   Of course, the corollary is also true: a diminishing tide lowers all the boats.   This is why, under the Obama Administration with its Keynesian economic policies more people are now dependent upon food stamps and other forms of government assistance.

- Obamacare was another hope and change achievement (without a single Republican vote in either the House or the Senate). What made the hair on the back of my neck stand up during his March 22, 2010 (11:47 EDT) victory speech[145] was when he said two things: first, "change in this country comes not from the top

---

[142] Veronique de Rugy, "The Facts about Stimulus Spending," Reason.com, July 8, 2011. Available at http://reason.com/archives/2011/07/08/the-facts-about-stimulus-spend

[143] Doug Bandow, "Federal Spending: Killing the Economy with Government Stimulus," Forbes.com, August 6, 2012. Available at http://www.forbes.com/sites/dougbandow/2012/08/06/federal-spending-killing-the-economy-with-government-stimulus/

[144] This axiom was part of a speech given at the dedication of Greers Ferry Dam on October 3, 1963. Kennedy understood the delicate partnership between public and private sectors in growing and sustaining healthy economies. The speech is available at http://www.presidency.ucsb.edu/ws/index.php?pid=9455

[145] For a transcript of the speech see http://www.whitehouse.gov/the-press-office/remarks-president-house-vote-health-insurance-reform

down, but from the bottom up"--even though the majority of Americans were not in favor of this particular comprehensive bill; and, second, when Obama paused and looked straight into the camera (at about six minutes and seven seconds into the speech), saying, "This is what change looks like." President Obama clearly proclaimed to all Americans that he had every intention to push his progressive agenda. [146] He reiterated this intention in his "The Country We Believe In," speech on April 13, 2011 (see the transcript of this speech at Appendix A). As a modern grand inquisitor (see the "Dry, Parched Lips" conversation on September 23, 2012), President Obama, cheered on by progressives who currently have political power at the federal level, disregarded what the majority of Americans want. And even though Obama campaigned on themes of civility and bipartisanship, there was nothing civil or bipartisan about the tactics involved in passing the stimulus and healthcare acts.

Old Gadfly: Perhaps President Obama is demonstrating visionary leadership by pushing reform that may not be popular now but would make life better for more people over all in the future?

IM: First, for now, Americans live in a Constitutional Republic. We, the people, elect officials to represent us in matters of governance. All elected officials serve the will of the people, not the other way around. Yet, the President and the Democratic Party in Congress pushed policy that was not desired by the majority of the people. Second, in Obama's UN speech, he also cautioned about cracking down on dissent. Yet, unknown to most Americans, President Obama signed a unique provision into law in the recent National Defense Authorization Act--the power to arrest and detain American citizens indefinitely without trial. This news was not reported in the American mainstream media. I found it in *The Guardian*, a British newspaper.[147] Publicly, Obama claimed he would veto the Act if it contained the provision. In private, however, Obama threatened Congress that he would veto the Act if the detention provision was not included.[148]

---

[146] To observe the recorded speech, see
http://www.youtube.com/watch?v=GALYnnAQFKA

[147] Jonathan Turley, "The NDAA's Historic Assault on American Liberty," The Guardian, January 2, 2012. Available at
http://www.theguardian.com/commentisfree/cifamerica/2012/jan/02/ndaa-historic-assault-american-liberty

[148] Senator Carl Levin made Obama's duplicitous action public on the Senate floor. See the CSPA-2 video recording of this announcement at
http://www.youtube.com/watch?feature=endscreen&NR=1&v= xObDStJBDzc

This is a blatant example of duplicity. About this time, the Federal Emergency Management Agency (FEMA) solicited contractor bids for containment camps (five per state) to be established within 72 hours for camp populations up to 1,000 inhabitants per five acres in all 50 states.[149] Even the progressive Rachel Maddow of *MSNBC* expressed concerns.[150] And, amazingly, our President claims to have the power to assassinate American citizens, without due process.[151]

Old Gadfly: I remember when we made such a big deal about waterboarding. If I had a choice, I'd clearly take waterboarding over death by drone. Yet, to be frank, IM, I don't see anything so far that seems out of the ordinary for Washington, DC. How does this relate to engineering public sentiment?

IM: I'm just getting warmed up, Gadfly. As I casually observed actions and behaviors that seemed somewhat isolated from each other, I also kept hearing in the back of my mind: drip, drip, drip. Then, these seemingly isolated drops began to merge into a stream with force and direction. I pulled my copy of George Orwell's *1984* (with John Hurt and Richard Burton) off the shelf and inserted it into my DVD player. At the very beginning of the movie was a black screen, then these words in white:

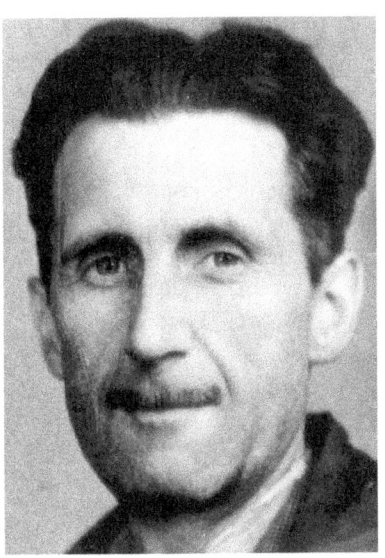

"WHO CONTROLS THE PAST CONTROLS THE FUTURE

---

149 Alan P. Halbert, "New Nationwide FEMA Camps Should Raise Eyebrows," American Thinker, January 2, 2012, Available at http://www.americanthinker.com/2012/01/new_nationwide_fema_camps_should _raise_eyebrows.html

150 Rachel Maddow, "Obama Justifies FEMA Imprisonment of Civilians," *MSNBC*, January 22, 2011. Video clip is available at http://www.youtube.com/watch?v=8mPZlysCAm0&feature=related

151 Jonathan Turley, "So, Eric Holder, We Should Just Trust that the President Won't Assassinate Us?" *The Guardian*, March 6, 2012. Available at http://www.theguardian.com/commentisfree/cifamerica/2012/mar/06/ eric-holder-trust-targeted-assassination

(Following a short pause, the next two lines appeared on the screen)

WHO CONTROLS THE PRESENT
CONTROLS THE PAST

This is when I truly understood the magnitude and danger of Obama and the progressive movement's design for engineering public sentiment. Unfortunately, many of our younger voters have no idea that Orwell was capturing the real dangers he actually witnessed in the Soviet Union and Germany when he wrote the original book in 1949.

Old Gadfly: IM, you are starting to frighten me. Didn't Lenin and Hitler promise hope and change?

IM: Yes, Lenin and Hitler did inspire the masses with promises of hope and change. In Lenin's case, change was revolution (from capitalism to socialism, as a transitory stage toward communism) and the promise was shared freedom and shared prosperity. Hitler promised to restore the dignity and esteem of the German population through massive changes in government administration and cultural norms (political correctness) following the harsh and demeaning consequences of the Versailles Treaty after World War I.

Old Gadfly: How did people buy into these promises?

IM: The people were agitated. Lenin and Hitler were able to create public narratives to rally the people against "perceived enemies" such as the bourgeoisie and Jews.

Old Gadfly: Do you think people anticipated the unintended consequences of the hope and change?

IM: Perhaps many did but felt powerless to do anything about it. This is why it is important for American citizens, right now, to take a closer look at what is going on in America. Clearly, those who control the present control the past, and by engineering sentiment about the past (even the

78

recent, nearly four dismal years of a sluggish domestic economy, not to mention foreign policy failures), they control the future.

Old Gadfly: Who do you mean by "those who control the present" and how do they do this?

IM: "Those" are the progressive politicians who currently control the federal government (and to a certain extent state, county, and municipal governments, given the extent of unionization), the mainstream media, academia, and Hollywood. Let me give some examples. Obama brings a philosophy and unique set of experiences into his governing style. He was

inspired by Saul Alinsky.[152] So was Hillary Clinton.[153] While husband Bill was President, Wellesley College was pressured[154] not to make public her thesis on Alinsky.[155] Alinsky was a University of Chicago-educated radical of the 60s and 70s. He wrote a book in 1971, *Rules for Radicals: A Pragmatic Primer for Realistic Radicals.* Alinsky gave a special acknowledgement to the one who inspired him: Lucifer, who, according to Alinsky, was a radical in his own right, winning his own kingdom from God himself.[156]

Alinsky also explained the rationale for his approach: (a) the masses must be made to feel frustrated, defeated, lost, and futureless, and thus ready to let go of the past; and (b) attitudes must be shaped in such a way as to be passive and non-challenging

[152] "Saul Alinsky, The Man Who Inspired Obama," *NPR*, January 30, 2009. Available at http://www.npr.org/ templates/story/story.php?storyId=100057050

[153] Peter Slevin, "For Clinton and Obama, a Common Ideological Touchstone," *The Washington Post*, March 25, 2007. Available at http://www.washingtonpost.com/wp-dyn/content/article/2007/03/24/AR2007032401152.html

[154] Bill Dedman, "Hillary's Thesis," *NBCNews.com*, September 6, 2007. Available at http://www.nbcnews.com/id/17388394/ns/politics-decision_08/t/how-clintons-wrapped-hillarys-thesis/

[155] Hillary Clinton's thesis paper on Saul Alinsky is available at http://www.hillaryclintonquarterly.com/ documents/HillaryClintonThesis.pdf

[156] Saul Alinsky, *Rules for Radicals: A Pragmatic Primer for Realistic Radicals*, (New York, NY: Vintage Books, 1972), p. xii.

toward change.[157] Of course, there must be the visible radical in which the masses place their trust in making any change. This sounds a lot like the hope and change slogan of the Obama campaign.

Further, Alinsky was very transparent in his goal: to change the world from what it is to what the radicals believe it should be. His book was written to provide tactics to make this happen, but more specifically to show Have-Nots how to take power away from the Haves.[158] Tellingly, Alinsky was not focused on improving quality of life. He, like Lucifer, sought power--his so called Have-Nots were mere pawns (or Mill's human instruments) in his political and social engineering chess game.

Old Gadfly: While Alinsky advanced his goal from an apparent idealistic perspective, I can see the danger of unintended consequences.

IM: What is disinguous about Alinsky's assertion is that Machiavelli described how princes managed power in competition with other princes in an international system, similar to the way prince Obama attempts to manage or balance power with princes in Russia, China, Iran, or the Middle East. From a practical standpoint, Alinsky presented tactics for taking away power in the form of rules. I'll single out four of the 13 to demonstrate how they are used in the current state of affairs.

- RULE 5: *"Ridicule is man's most potent weapon."*[159] It is nearly impossible to counterattack ridicule, and it angers the opposition. This anger then causes the ridiculed to react to the ridiculer, who maintains the advantage. Recall the rampant ridiculing of Sarah Palin, or even more recently, Clint Eastwood.

- RULE 8: *"Keep the pressure on."*[160] In other words, ridicule is a campaign approach, with different tactics and actions that draw upon any and all events of the period for the attacker's purpose. Truthfulness is not a required condition. Events need not be true; they can be manufactured. Remember Senator Harry Reid's comment about Mitt Romney not paying taxes for 10 years?[161] While not true, the comment was political noise that generated mainstream media news cycles. In another example, rule 8

---

[157] Ibid, p. xix.

[158] Ibid, p. 3.

[159] Ibid, p. 128.

[160] Ibid.

[161] Sam Stein and Ryan Grim, "Harry Reid: Bain Investor Told Me that Mitt Romney 'Didn't Pay any Taxes for 10 Years,'" *The Huffington Post*, July 31, 2012. Available at http://www.huffingtonpost.com/2012/07/31/ harry-reid-romney-taxes_n_1724027.html

delivered great results in the state of Colorado. See Fred Barnes' analysis of these tactics in his article, "The Colorado Model."[162] The key point of Barnes's article is that most Americans are completely unaware of the integrated, behind the scenes efforts to create political noise through allegations that do not need to be true. These allegations start news cycles with mainstream media and sidetrack Republican campaigns with the time and cost of legal defenses.[163]

- o A recognized master of this particular tactic is David Axelrod. Axelrod has made a lot of money for his public relations firm by engineering public (and decision-maker) sentiment through a method called astro-turfing.[164]
- o Another professional tactician of rule 8 is David Corn of *Mother Jones*. Corn is a political activist masquerading as a journalist. Corn is the one who generated news cycles with Romney's 47% comments.[165]
- o Corn also generated the news cycles that prompted the Valerie Plame federal investigation.[166] The problem with the

---

[162] Fred Barnes, "The Colorado Model: The Democrats' Plan for Turning Red States Blue," *The Weekly Standard*, July 21, 2008. Available at http://www.weeklystandard.com/Content/Public/Articles/000/000 /015/316nfdzw.asp

[163] See Amanda Carpenter, "Gov. Sarah Palin Quietly Cleared of All Ethics Charges," The Washington Times, June 8, 2009; available at http://www.newsmax.com/InsideCover/palin-charges-dismissed/2009/06/08/id/ 330768. See also "Ethics Complaints Filed against Palin," *The Anchorage Daily News*, June 21, 2009; available at http://www.adn.com/2009/06/21/838912/ethics-complaints-filed-against.html. See also Becky Bohrer, "Judge Formally Tosses Juneau Man's Lawsuit against Palin," *The Anchorage Daily News*, October 2, 2012; available at http://www.adn.com/2012/10/02/2647793/judge-formally-tosses-juneau-mans.html. See also

[164] Howard Wolinsky, "The Secret Side of David Axelrod," *Bloomberg Businessweek*, March 14, 2008. Available at http://www.businessweek.com/stories/2008-03-14/the-secret-side-of-david-axelrodbusinessweek-business-news-stock-market-and-financial-advice

[165] David Weigel, "What Did David Corn Know, and When Did He Know It?" *Slate*, September 19, 2012. Available at http://www.slate.com/blogs/weigel/2012/09/19/mother_jones_tape_conservativ e_accuse_ magazine_ of_unfair_editing.html

[166] David Corn, "Nigergate Thuggery," *The Nation*, August 4, 2003. Available at http://www.thenation.com/ article/nigergate-thuggery#

supposed "Plamegate scandal" is that there was a deliberate attempt by Valerie Plame and her husband, Ambassador Joseph Wilson, to undermine the Bush Administration's claim that Saddam Hussein wanted to acquire "uranium yellow cake"--material used to make nuclear weapons. There is some evidence that Plame, who was a weapons of mass destruction (WMD) analyst with the CIA, had a major hand in getting her husband appointed by the CIA to travel to Niger in late February 2002 to see if there had been any attempt by Hussein to purchase yellow cake.[167] Wilson's ego would not settle for simply reporting back to the CIA. He drew tremendous attention to himself when he convinced *The New York Times* to publish his article, "What I Didn't Find in Africa" on July 6, 2003.[168] The article was very bold, essentially accusing President Bush and his Administration of deliberately misleading the public. This article was followed a week later on July 14, 2003 by Robert Novak in *The Washington Post*. Novak's article, "Mission to Niger," connected Ambassador Wilson to a member within the CIA that facilitated the trip: his wife, Valerie Plame.[169] This led to a news cycle firestorm and public outrage. How could the Bush Administration, the target of the Alinsky Rule 5 tactic, defend itself with an explanation for how the Wilson trip actually came to be? But, once momentum developed in left-leaning mainstream media news cycles, Bush felt compelled to appoint a federal prosecutor. In doing so, Bush did something Obama refuses to do for any of the many potential illegal activities under his Administration--such as Fast & Furious, Solyndra, and other green energy failures.[170] But, then again, despite nearly singular efforts on

---

[167] Given that the summary and analysis provided is well substantiated with links to original sources, I highly recommend "Plame Affair" at *Wikipedia*: http://en.wikipedia.org/wiki/Valerie_Plame_scandal

[168] Joseph C. Wilson IV, "What I Didn't Find in Africa: Did the Bush Administration Manipulate Intelligence about Saddam Hussein's Weapons Program to Justify an Invasion of Iraq?" *The New York Times*, July 6, 2003. Available at http://www.nytimes.com/2003/07/06/opinion/06WILS.html

[169] Robert Novak, "Mission to Niger," *The Washington Post*, July 14, 2003. Available at

[170] When this conversation took place, the Benghazi incident, the IRS targeting of conservative groups, and the Justice Department's harassment of journalists and news organizations had yet to take place.

the part of *Fox News*, Obama has not been pressured by the left-leaning news media calling for accountability. Nonetheless, after countless depositions and testimonials before a grand jury, Scooter Libby (advisor to Vice President Dick Cheney) became the smoking gun and was convicted for obstruction of justice and perjury, sentenced to 30 months of jail and fined $250,000.[171] Yet, there was absolutely no interest or concern that the individual who actually "leaked" Valerie Plame's identity to Robert Novak and precipitated the investigation was the Deputy Secretary of State, Richard Armitage (left frame in picture below).[172] Colin Powell (right frame in picture below), the sitting Secretary of State and a favorite of the left-leaning

mainstream media, was at odds with the rest of Bush's national security team (Vice President Dick Cheney, Secretary of Defense Donald Rumsfeld, and National Security Advisor Condoleezza Rice); so, the left-leaning news media had no interest in being critical of Powell's number two man. Scooter Libby became the sacrificial lamb and a victory for the progressive movement's effort to shape a public narrative to paint, in the minds of the American public, a corrupted Bush Administration. Armitage

---

[171] "Libby Sentenced to 30 Months in Prison," *NBCNews.com*, June 5, 2007. Available at http://www. nbcnews. com/id/19039377/

[172] Neil A. Lewis, "Source of C.I.A. Leak Said to Admit Role," *The New York Times*, August 30, 2006. Available at http://www.nytimes.com/2006/08/30/washington/30armitage.html?_r=0

spinelessly slouched into the private sector, untouched by the firestorm he precipitated. Perhaps on another day, I can offer my analysis of how Colin Powell, a once widely respected and admired public servant, became afflicted by the insidious and corruptive manifestations of political progressivism. Meanwhile, I want to now discuss another Alinsky rule.

- RULE 12: *"The price of a successful attack is a constructive alternative."*[173] This means to be on guard for a sudden agreement by the opponent. Essentially, the attacker must maneuver to place the opponent in a position to be vulnerable to be attacked by asking for an alternative to what has just been agreed upon, such as a proposal as to how to implement an agreed upon demand--again, conflict must remain in effect with the opponent. Two relatively recent examples demonstrate this tactic.
  o The first involved the debt issue. Obama could not afford to revisit this issue before the 2012 election. Bob Woodward provides an account of the standoff in an excerpt to his book, *The Price of Politics*.[174] Obama and his lieutenants had to keep control of the debt ceiling crisis, even though Senator Reid presented a bipartisan solution to the issue. This solution was shot down and Obama called for an alternative solution. Ironically, Diane Sawyer on the *ABC Nightly News* managed to shape an interview with Woodward on this issue in such a way as to elevate Obama's success in managing the debt crisis on a scale of Kennedy's Cuban Missile Crisis.[175] The framing of this interview is a blatant example of mendacity, complicity, and duplicity. Unfortunately, attempts to inform the public with more

[173] Alinsky, p. 131.

[174] Bob Woodward, "Inside Story of Obama's Struggle to Keep Congress from Controlling Outcome of Debt Ceiling Crisis," The Washington Post, September 8, 2012. Available at http://www.washingtonpost.com/ politics/a-president-sidelined/2012/09/08/a463793c-f6db-11e1-8253-3f495ae70650_story.html

[175] Diane Sawyer, "What Went Wrong on Failed Debt Deal," *ABC News*, September 10, 2012. Available at http://abcnews.go.com/Politics/video/woodward-bob-sawyer-diane-exclusive-debt-author-book-tax-politics-us-17198306

objective views from other news sources get drowned out by the left-leaning pro-Obama mainstream media.[176]

o The second example involves how Obama and Democrats provided a constructive alternative involving the payroll tax holiday in order to manipulate the public narrative. On December 20, 2011, I caught a headline on page A23 of *The New York Times*: "House Republicans Refuse to Budge on Extension of Payroll Tax Cut" (the online heading was "House Set to Vote Down Payroll Tax Extension.")[177] The article commends the Democrat-controlled Senate for exercising leadership and advancing a solution, and harshly criticizes the Republican-led House for being obstinate. **What the article does not say** is that House Republicans had already forwarded a bill, passed on December 13. House Resolution (H.R.) 3630, "Temporary Payroll Tax Cut Continuation Act of 2011," passed with 224 Republicans and 10 Democrats voting in favor, and 14 Republicans and 179 Democrats voting against the bill. **H.R. 3630 provided for a 12-month payroll tax cut.** On December 17, the Senate sent Senate Amendment 146 to the House, an amendment to H.R. 3630 that changed the 12-month payroll tax cut to *2 months*. Yet, *The New York Times* headline and content made it look like Republicans blocked the payroll tax cut. Why would the Democrat-controlled Senate not approve the House bill? I offer three reasons: (a) Democrats could not afford to let the public narrative suggest Republicans are interested in helping the middle class; (b) President Obama and other Democrat politicians need this issue to support their middle class warrior strategy against the wealthy; and (c) Obama and Democrats count on mainstream media complicity in shaping public narratives through duplicitous

---

[176] Mary Kate Cary, "Americans Are Sick of Media's Pro-Obama Bias," U.S. News & World Report, September 21, 2012. Available at http://www.usnews.com/opinion/blogs/mary-kate-cary/2012/09/21/ americans-are-sick-of-medias-pro-obama-bias

[177] Jennifer Steinhauer and Robert Pear, "House Set to Vote Down Payroll Tax Extension," *The New York Times*, December 20, 2011. Available at http://www.nytimes.com/2011/12/20/us/politics/house-set-to-vote-down-payroll-tax-cut-extension.html?src=un&feedurl=http%3A%2F%2Fjson8.nytimes.com%252%20Fpages%2Fpolitics%2Findex.jsonp&gwh=5C8D63090F9E5332654370A813E72A25

and mendacious articles such as this one on the pay-roll tax legislative efforts. Now, I'll move on to the last and most dangerous Alinsky rule.

- RULE 13: *"Pick the target, freeze it, personalize it, and polarize it."*[178] While Romney and his affiliates have produced negative ads about Obama policies and performance, they have not gone after Obama as a person. Obama on the other hand is deliberately exploiting rule 13. He is fully aware of this, but still chooses to play by Alinsky philosophy and tactics because the end justifies the means, even if the means are immoral.
  - o Obama admitted to such tactics in an interview segment not aired on Sunday's (September 23, 2012) *60 Minutes*.[179] Obama admitted political ads "went overboard" but were justified to amplify differences between himself and Romney.
  - o Further, someday, history will more objectively record how George Bush was a target and victim of rule 13. Obama continues to blame today's lack of economic recovery on Bush policies. He even suggests Romney wants to take America back to the policies that caused the economic mess we're still experiencing, despite analysis strongly suggesting other causes for the economic crisis, as we discussed in a previous conversation.[180]
  - o In another example, once the Tea Party was sufficiently excoriated in the mainstream media, it was relatively easy to target individuals affiliated with the Tea Party. These individuals are labeled, "extremists." Yet, if one were to really look at the core principles of the Tea Party movement, he or she would see that members of the Tea Party are not anti-government--most of them are hard-working middle class Americans who are completely in favor of paying reasonable taxes to support a limited government. They are concerned about a government that is (a) too large and unsustainable; and (b) too egalitarian in taking away

---

[178] Alinsky, op cit, p. 131.

[179] "Unaired Excerpts from the Obama, Romney Interviews," *60 Minutes*, September 23, 2012. Available at http://www.cbsnews.com/8334-504803_162-57518524-10391709/unaired-excerpts-from-the-obama-romney-interviews/?pageNum=10&tag=next

[180] Old Gadfly, "The 'Inherited Economy' Narrative," *Gadfly Corner*, August 16, 2012. Available at http://gadflycorner.blogspot.com/2012/08/the-inherited-economy-narrative.html

freedoms (or property, such as earned income) from some to promote equality for others (redistribution of wealth). Thus, members of the Tea Party believe the recent political direction and actions of the Obama Administration appear to clearly demonstrate what Jefferson cautioned against in the Declaration of Independence:

> whenever any Form of Government becomes destructive of these ends, it is the Right of the People to alter or to abolish it, and to institute new Government, laying its foundation on such principles and organizing its powers in such form, as to them shall seem most likely to effect their Safety and Happiness. Prudence, indeed, will dictate that Governments long established should not be changed for light and transient causes; and accordingly all experience hath shewn, that mankind are more disposed to suffer, while evils are sufferable, than to right themselves by abolishing the forms to which they are accustomed. But when a long train of abuses and usurpations, pursuing invariably the same Object evinces a design to reduce them under absolute Despotism, it is their right, it is their duty, to throw off such Government, and to provide new Guards for their future security.

By today's progressive definitions, Thomas Jefferson would be called an extremist.

Old Gadfly: But perhaps we live in different circumstances than in Jefferson's time.

IM: While technology is the largest difference over time, human nature is human nature. Orwell understood this. In *Animal Farm*, written in the 1940s, Orwell describes a fictional administrative state led by Napoleon (modeled after Joseph Stalin). Napoleon rallied the animals

around a symbolic windmill (i.e., green energy) to keep them distracted from other administrative failures. In time, the administrative regime devolved into mere totalitarianism when the government could no longer deliver on promises. The government's original seven commandments (e.g., politically correct norms) were reduced to one: all animals are created equal; some are more equal than others. While the book was fictional, Orwell's concern flowed from emerging political economic ideologies that believed in the hubris of capitalism, the efficiencies of statism, and the intellectual idealism of socialism. These same tenets define today's American progressive movement. The outcome of this movement, if left unchecked, will be the same as in *Animal Farm,* and the actual fate of the former Soviet Union, Hitler's Germany, and Mussolini's Italy.

Old Gadfly: Americans should have enough power and common sense to do something in the November elections. But, how would you convince them that Romney is a better choice?

IM: Unlike your optimism in Americans having common sense, Bill Maher, an outspoken progressive, believes they're stupid.[181] I do not. Like you, I have confidence that Americans can do the right thing. To our fellow Americans, I would say, "imagine this: If Obama is reelected, then he would consider this a *fait accompli* mandate to continue his current policies. When the debt inevitably continues to grow with no economic growth to sustain it, and in order to avoid a Greek-style collapse, the Administration will first seize the trillions of dollars corporations are still holding back while hoping for a more certain business climate, and then the Administration will seize personal retirement accounts. Yes, IRAs, 401Ks, and so forth. Keep in mind, of the trillions of dollars already collected for Social Security and Medicare, politicians have already spent it—todays benefits reflect borrowed money. What makes you think they would not spend other wealth that they can seize for political purposes?"

This is not conspiracy theory. After all, as George Lakoff tells us in *Whose Freedom,* wealth in America belongs to the commonwealth. He actually believes America's founders fully intended to pool the common wealth for the common good; in other words the government is needed to control and administer the "common wealth" for the benefit of all.[182]

Old Gadfly: Won't the American people protest?

IM: Yes, if they can overcome the human bondage of emotion. Obama's likeability index appears to be more compelling than actual facts and what they mean. But, the Administration has already anticipated the possibility of protest--this is why Obama has already put in place, as we have already discussed, the authority to detain American citizens indefinitely in statewide FEMA camps, or even to assassinate those he deems a real

---

[181] Bill Maher, "America Is Stupid," *CNN.com,* July 27, 2009. Available at http://www.youtube.com/watch?v=r WWHHNeGMss

[182] Lakoff, *Whose Liberty,* op cit., pp. 155-156.

threat to security. Sounds like a dream, doesn't it? It can happen. It has happened. But, remember, those who control the present are working hard to control what we know about the past in order to control the future. And when the end (i.e., control of the future) justifies the means, mendacity, complicity, and duplicity are not considered immoral behaviors.

Old Gadfly: IM, your analysis is very discouraging. And, while I'd like to find a way to soften the harsh reality we've embraced in this conversation, I cannot help but recall something I read a few years ago. In 1985, Neil Postman published a book, *Amusing Ourselves to Death*. In the Foreword to his book, Postman observed that the year 1984 came but Orwell's prophecy did not. [183] The reason for this, he believed, was the enduring strength of the roots of liberal democracy. Postman went on to suggest that while Orwell's dark vision of Big Brother did not happen, Aldous Huxley's prophecy in *Brave New World* did. Huxley, according to Postman, believed people would easily accept oppression because of the access to so many distractions and pleasures (e.g., some equivalent of the feelies, the orgy porgy, and the centrifugal bumblepuppy), many of these tied to technology. Technologies will diminish their capacity to think.

IM: An Obama reelection will be additional proof that Postman foresaw such an outcome 27 years ago. If so, perhaps we can only console ourselves with the wisdom of Ecclesiastes 1:2-4, about the futility of vanity and any profit from our labor since one generation passes and another comes in a world that is far more enduring than any single generation.

Old Gadfly: Very deep, IM. Shall we have a glass of wine before we're offered hemlock from the Obama Administration?

---

[183] Neil Postman, *Amusing Ourselves to Death: Public Discourse in the Age of Show Business*, (New York, NY: Penguin Books, 1986), pp. xix-xx.

9 MEMETICS AND POLITICS

October 18, 2012
The Coffee Cup Café, Monument, Colorado

Old Gadfly: IM, what did you think about the second presidential debate (October 16, 2012)?

IM: It was certainly more competitive than the first one. But, I must say that it also manifested some of the effects of engineering public sentiment that we talked about in our last conversation.

Old Gadfly: How so?

IM: There were elements of the debate that stemmed from and contributed to a relatively obscure concept called memes. Richard Dawkins introduced the concept of memes in his 1976 book, *The Selfish Gene*. Memes are transmitted through a process of imitation from person to person and essentially are the building blocks of human culture. Memes can represent ideas, concepts, beliefs, fashions, techniques, interpretations of phenomena, and other forms of cognitions. A meme can be false; yet, unchallenged false memes can still be rapidly propagated within a culture. Richard Brodie wrote an entire book to drive this point home in *Virus of the Mind: The New Science of the Meme*. Genes are to genetics as memes are to memetics.

Old Gadfly: Fascinating, IM. Tell me how memes were present in the debate.

IM: The first major indication was how President Obama characterized Governor Romney's economic plan. Obama asserted Romney's plan would cost $5 trillion for proposed across the board 20% tax cuts, another $2 trillion for additional military programs, and another trillion to continue Bush tax cuts for the wealthiest Americans for a total of $8 trillion.

Old Gadfly: Maybe he's correct.

IM: Gadfly, when Obama says "cost," he makes it sound like the government will be paying $6 trillion to Americans. When he says it will cost $5 trillion for across the board tax cuts and $1 trillion to the wealthiest Americans, he implies that these people will receive money from the federal government. What is really happening is that the tax policy would not take $6 trillion from the earned incomes of Americans. There is no cost to the government. It's just $6 trillion less than those in the federal government can get to spend on programs and services. Let me give you an analogy. I want to buy a $30,000 Lexus but need a loan to pay for it. If the bank denies me the loan, then the bank is "costing" me $30,000 that I need to buy the car. We know this is not true. Here's a different analogy closet to Obama's imagination. I want to feed the hungry in Monument but need $30,000 to carry out the program I imagine would do this. I go to neighbors and ask that they contribute to the $30,000 program. None are willing to do this. Are they costing my program $30,000?

Old Gadfly: Language does matter.

IM: Obama claimed his own policies would cut deficits in half and restore unemployment rates below 6% during his first term. His policies failed to do this; yet, Obama claims he needs another four years to give his same policies time to work. This is the same man that thinks he can lecture a man who actually has a successful economic and business track record. But, Obama is clever. By the way, I almost said smart; but a smart person might make an adjustment when things aren't working. Obama knows enough people will resonate with the $8 trillion cost. The $8 trillion idea is a meme that will get transmitted to others. It took nanoseconds with the pundits at *MSNBC News* following the debate.

Old Gadfly: Your argument is plausible, and it sounds like you have more evidence to discuss.

IM: Another example was town hall participant Susan Katz's question:

> Governor Romney, I am an undecided voter, because I'm disappointed with the lack of progress I've seen in the last four years. However, I do attribute much of America's economic and international problems to the failings and missteps of the Bush administration. Since both you and President Bush are Republicans, I fear a return to the policies of those years should you win this election. What is the biggest difference between you and George W. Bush, and how do you differentiate yourself from George W. Bush?

Gadfly, what do you think is the message in this question?

Old Gadfly: That today's economic and international problems were caused by Bush Administration policies.

IM: Exactly! What you just described is considered a meme because it has been propagated in the public narrative, treated as an indisputable fact, and internalized in the American culture. Do you believe it is true?

Old Gadfly: There may be some elements of truth to the meme.

IM: Name one.

Old Gadfly: One common argument is that Bush tax cuts led to reduced tax revenues and corresponding annual deficits. But, we already examined this argument in a previous conversation: tax cuts actually corresponded with significant increases in tax revenue between 2004 and 2007. And, as Governor Romney tried to explain, when he was allowed to speak, tax cuts can lead to job creation. Between 2004 and 2007 unemployment rates decreased from 6.0% to 4.6%. But, then we saw a decline in tax revenue and a rising unemployment rate in 2008. What do you believe accounts for these developments?

IM: Gadfly, we talked about these developments in a previous conversation ("Tax Cuts, Unemployment, and Public Debt," August 26, 2012). Between 2004 and 2008, there were no change in tax rates, but there was a major shift in political power from Republican to Democrat in both houses of Congress. Also, the burst of the housing bubble in 2008 resulted from subprime mortgages and Democrat legislation (i.e., the Federal Housing Enterprises Financial Safety and Soundness Act of 1992). Remember, we also discussed the anti-business ratings by the Chamber of Commerce for both Harry Reid in the Senate and Nancy Pelosi in the House.

Old Gadfly: Is there *any* evidence to support the Bushonomics meme?

IM: In probably *the best* attempt to justify the Bushonomics meme, the Center for American Progress published a white paper in August 2008 by Scott Lilly, "Understanding Bushonomics: How We Got into This Mess in the First Place."[184] The paper singled out taxes, minimum wage, trade, unions, and immigration policies. Let me critique the paper's arguments:

- One paragraph on tax policy presented an argument that the wealthiest received a much greater tax cut than middle income families. The argument wants the reader to believe the government is giving more to the wealthy than to the middle

---

[184] Scott Lilly, "Understanding Bushonomics: How We Got into This Mess in the First Place," Center for American Progress, August 2008. Available at http://www.americanprogress.org/issues/open-government/report/2008/08/04/4763/understanding-bushonomics/

class. Taxes take money away from those who have earned it. So, in reality tax cuts take less from those who earned it. Many of the "wealthy" took the tax reduction and invested it. The investment created jobs, which in turn increased the tax base. This is why the tax cuts lowered the unemployment rate between 2004 and 2007 and actually generated more tax revenue for government budgets. And, don't forget, even with the Bush tax cuts, the top 5% still pay 60% of the tax burden.

- The paper provided three paragraphs to demonize President Bush on the minimum wage. Lilly presumes a minimum wage increases benefits for lower-skilled, lower-paid workers despite evidence of the unintended consequences of a mandated minimum wage increase (i.e., those it targets for the benefit are most vulnerable to losing their jobs because employers will keep more experienced people with a smaller pay increase while letting go the less experienced, lowest paid employees).[185] Lilly acknowledges that even though Bush did not directly oppose adjustments to the minimum wage, a veto threat tied any increase to business tax cuts. The amazing dynamic here is that the progressive view believes government knows better than the private sector regarding how to grow the economy. In doing so, the government issues rules and regulations to control centers of production (sounds like the former Soviet Union). What progressives either do not understand, or dismiss as a fact that does not fit their narrative frame, is that when certain wages became too high in relation to globalized market forces, many jobs, such as manufacturing, migrated to foreign economies that are a better fit. Ironically, the Obama Administration is now trying to entice the manufacturing sector to bring jobs back to America--incentives that include tax cuts.[186]

---

[185] See Daniel Aaronson and Eric French, "Product Market Evidence on the Employment Effects of the Minimum Wage," *Journal of Labor Economics*, 25(1) (January 2007), pp. 167-200. Using the restaurant industry as the sample population, Aaronson and French concluded that "a 10% increase in the minimum wage lowers low-skill employment by 2% - 4% and total restaurant employment by 1% - 3%. See also, Sara Lemos, "A Survey of the Effects of the Minimum Wage on Prices," *Journal of Economic Surveys*, 22(1) (February 2008), pp. 187-212.

[186] See Mark Landler, "Obama Calls for Tax Breaks to Return Jobs from Abroad," *The New York Times*, January 11, 2012. Retrieved on June 10, 2012 from http://www.nytimes.com/2012/01/12/business/obama-seeks-tax-breaks-to-return-jobs-from-abroad.html; see also Christopher Power, "Do Tax Breaks Help Manufacturers?" *Bloomberg Business Week Asia*, February 24, 2012, retrieved on June 10 from http://www.businessweek.com/articles/2012-02-24/do-tax-breaks-help-

- Lilly then claimed Bush trade policies led to a tripling (by a factor of 3.1) of the bilateral trade deficit with China between 2000 and 2007 (from $83 billion to over $258 billion). This snapshot provides no context for the broader trend that preceded Bush's tenure. During the Clinton Administration, the trade deficit more than quadrupled (by a factor of 4.5, from $18.3 billion to $83 billion).[187]

- Related to the trade policies, Lilly reported a loss of 21% or 3.7 million manufacturing jobs between 2000 and 2008--jobs that migrated to foreign countries. This change reflects a corresponding loss in union membership in the manufacturing sector, from 14.8% to 11.4%, or a loss of 30% of union members.[188] These numbers reflect the unsustainable expectations and cost of union membership in a globalized economy.

- Lilly suggested Bush may have contributed to illegal immigration, not from any specific policy, but from association with industrial sectors that hired illegal immigrants, such as restaurants, construction, and so forth. The evidence Lilly presented comes from political campaign contributions in the 2006 election cycle from OpenSecrets.org. And, he is correct. Yet, two years later, political campaign contributions from many of the same sectors shifted toward the Obama campaign.[189] Thus, Lilly's suggestion that Bush policies exacerbated the illegal immigration issue simply has no logical foundation. What is more informative, however, is the realization that these business sectors place

---

manufacturers; see also Susan Helper, Timothy Krueger, and Howard Wial, (February 2012), *Why Does Manufacturing Matter? Which Manufacturing Matters? A Policy Framework*, Metropolitan Policy Program at Brookings, (Washington, DC: The Brookings Institute), retrieved on June 10 from http://www.brookings.edu/~/media/research/files/papers/2012/2/22%20 manufacturing%20helper%20krueger%20wial/0222_manufacturing_helper_krueger_wial.pdf

[187] See Trade Deficit Data for these periods from the U.S. Department of Commerce. Available at http://www.census.gov/foreign-trade/balance/c5700.html

[188] See the Annual Union Membership Report from the U.S. Bureau of Labor Statistics. Available at http://www.bls.gov/news.release/archives/union2_01232013.pdf

[189] See historical data for 2008 in "Misc Business," Open Secrets.org., available at http://www.opensecrets.org/ industries/indus.php?ind=N

greater faith in the Republican Party to promote business. Historical political campaign data support this notion.[190] Businesses in the private sector create jobs. Governments only create jobs in the public sector, which require additional resources from the private sector.

Recall our discussion about the burst of the housing bubble in 2008 ("The Art of Economy Surfing," September 7, 2012). The point I am making, Gadfly, is that the Bush Administration has been illogically, perhaps fraudulently, accused of causing the current economic situation.

Old Gadfly: So, the narrative advanced by a certain political faction has attempted to propagate a political bogeyman meme that may not be true.

IM: Exactly. The Bush Administration meme became a prima facie straw man for future political argument. This allowed then candidate Obama to repeatedly describe McCain as a Bush clone. Bush policies were bad, and McCain is like Bush; therefore, McCain is bad.

Old Gadfly: So, the question posed to Romney was really a conundrum--how is Governor Romney different from a false narrative? Knowing how complex the explanation is for today's economic situation, Romney had no reasonable alternative in responding to the question other than the way he did, which is unfortunate because the Bushonomics meme became further entrenched in the public narrative and the minds of Copernican drones.

IM: An objective media source should not have allowed this happen. Twenty years ago, the first news source I digested each day was the *New York Times*. At that time, the *New York Times* deserved the reputation as the bellwether news source--it was nonpartisan and objective. But, today, the *New York Times* seems to have taken on the role of a state-controlled news source, similar to the *Pravda* at the peak of the former Soviet Union.

Old Gadfly: I can see the role our media plays in propagating memes, whether true or false. How do you tie memes to politics?

IM: David Easton defined politics as the authoritative allocation of values.[191] The political strategy for presidential candidates is to demonstrate they have the best plan to advance values for the majority of Americans. Values then are advanced through policy and budgets.

Old Gadfly: What are American values?

---

[190] Ibid.

[191] David Easton, *The Political System: An Inquiry into the State of Political Science* (New York: Knopf, 1953), p. 139.

IM: Good question. Values once defined become memes that are dependent upon a medium for propagating them to other people. So, the questions important to understanding how this process works are: (a) who defines values; and (b) how are people within a society informed of these values? Political elite determine values. Government technocrats, academia, Hollywood, and the news media are sources and venues for propagating value-based memes.

Old Gadfly: Let's get more concrete in our discussion. Explain how the values of life and liberty are propagated within our society.

IM: You really know how to peel the onion, so to speak, Gadfly. Let me address liberty first. Conservatives believe in individual liberty, yet with a sense of civic responsibility to one's family, neighborhood, community, and other forms of association. Progressives, on the other hand, believe in collective liberty, that an individual depends upon others for safety and security and that political elite provide for these values. This is why progressives insist upon unions, and why unions heavily (nearly 100%) endorse and fund Democrat candidates. As we mentioned before, collective liberty was Hillary Rodham Clinton's thesis in her book, *It Takes a Village*. Amity Shlaes described progressive American fascination with the collective liberty experiments of Joseph Stalin and Adolph Hitler in Chapter 2 of her book, *The Forgotten Man*. Further, if you ever want to read a savvy, yet disturbing, display of language manipulation, read Professor George Lakoff's book, *Whose Liberty?* Lakoff believes no one pulls himself up by the bootstraps and that individually earned wealth belongs to the commonwealth. Finally, recall our discussion about the Grand Inquisitor parable. The Grand Inquisitor is today's progressive equivalent; whereas, conservatives are more consistent with the vision of Christ and the Judeo-Christian philosophy.

Old Gadfly: You describe a stark contrast between progressives and conservatives regarding liberty. Now, how about life?

IM: Conservatives are generally pro-life, which means that while they respect a woman's legal right to keep or abort a child, they are morally opposed to abortion because it is the taking of a life. Progressives, on the other hand, say that a woman's reproductive right, as a value, trumps the right to life of the baby in her womb.

Old Gadfly: IM, as a man, perhaps you don't understand a woman's dilemma when she finds herself to be pregnant.

IM: You raise an important point, Gadfly; and, this is an important reason not to judge the moral intentions of a woman. Yet, many decisions are made with incomplete information or as a result of the human bondage we discussed previously, where emotion trumps reason. Nonetheless, this abortion debate is where we have a moral obligation to judge the institutions and norms that shape our society and in turn some of the choices that are informed or not. Let me explain.

Context is important. First, with the exception of artificial insemination, pregnancies are caused by sexual activity between a man and a woman. This is an important point. Pregnancies are not like catching a cold or the flu, where some errant sperm cell just happened to find its way to an egg cell. According to Planned Parenthood's analytical think tank, the Guttmacher Institute, less than 1% of abortions are due to rape- or incest-related pregnancies. That means nearly 99% of abortions stem from consensual sexual activity. By the Institute's own account, more than 1.2 million abortions took place in America in 2006. This single-year number of 1.2 million abortions is more than the cumulative number of American casualties incurred in wars from the Revolutionary War to now.

Second, the meme, reproductive right, technically means the right to reproduce, and reproduction happens through sexual activity. If the meme, reproductive right, includes the right to kill an unborn child, regardless of the reason (e.g., unwanted, inconvenient, wrong gender, a male partner of dubious genetic stock, etc.), then a more descriptive term for the value would be the right of motherhood. This would more appropriately describe a woman's decision to be a mother to an unborn child, or not.

Third, the reproductive rights argument is a form of eugenics; whereby, a woman exercises a legal prerogative to manipulate nature's law. Both reasons are consistent with Margaret Sanger's vision for population control from a eugenics perspective. Eugenics was an attempt to reduce the number of lesser desirable human beings in favor of those from a more favorable genetic stock. This ideology was penetrating the United States by the same progressives who admired Stalin's and Hitler's experiments with collective liberty. This is why Sanger started the Planned Parenthood program, which to this day has facilities positioned in neighborhoods characterized by poor minority populations.[192] Sanger's worldview justified intellectuals, such as herself, with a moral obligation to rid the world of lesser desired human beings. Her biographical history is readily available in libraries and the Internet. Her legacy lives on with an even larger and more pervasive Planned Parenthood organization.

Fourth, while today's Planned Parenthood leaders tone down

---

[192] See well-cited background research at
http://www.citizenreviewonline.org/special_issues/population/
the_negro_project.htm; http://www.examiner.com/conservative-in-virginia-beach/planned-parenthood-is-the-black-community-s-worst-enemy;
http://www.washingtontimes.com/news/2008/aug/25/planned-parenthood-targets-blacks/; and http://bloodmoneyfilm.com/blog/planned-parenthood-eugenics

Sanger's rhetoric, the original mission remains the same. The insult to those who understand the genesis and mission of Planned Parenthood is that by paying their federal income tax, they have been co-opted in the eugenics model when the federal government subsidizes this enterprise with millions of dollars annually. This federal funding is an example of egalitarianism, a concept we discussed in a previous conversation.

Fifth, Planned Parenthood is a 501(c)(3) nonprofit organization. Perhaps it should seek the additional millions of dollars from private sector donors who believe in the ideology of eugenics. Today's Planned Parenthood champions would deny the above logic. They tell us they are in the practice of protecting a woman's reproductive health (and, incidentally, Planned Parenthood is an industry with jobs and income). Yet, they avoid discussing the one choice that puts health at risk, whether from a venereal disease or unwanted pregnancy: voluntary sexual activity. And of course, there is a related issue regarding employers (even religious ones) being legally mandated under the Affordable Care Act (Obamacare) to provide contraceptives and abortifacients to their employees, implying a statist encouragement of sexual activity. Does this sound like Huxley's vision in *A Brave New World* (i.e., feelies, the orgy porgy, and the centrifugal bumblepuppy)? Frankly, the Planned Parenthood legacy (and its support for sexual freedom without consequence) seems to be profoundly reflected in Proverbs 26:11, about dogs returning to their vomit as fools repeat their folly. Human nature is human nature. The Book of Proverbs is about 5000 years old, dating back to King Solomon and the Sumerian civilization (circa 3000 B.C).[193]

Old Gadfly: IM, your arguments are logical and compelling. What are the implications?

IM: Let me share two reflections. First, the sad part of the abortion experience in America, or anywhere in the world for that matter, is that many of these women find themselves in a situation of which they were not prepared, whether through ignorance, loneliness, or whatever reason that compelled them to engage in sexual activity. They then find too much encouragement from those they trust to encourage or guide them through an abortion. While many of those they trust encourage abortion out of compassion for the pregnant woman or girl, they fail to understand that the aborted child is not aborted from her memory. Years later, many of these women will be struck by the cold and ruthless act of abortion and will carry that scar forever.

Second, John Stuart Mill spoke of a profound metaphor when he said "When a people are used as mere human instruments for firing cannon

[193] Lawrence Boadt, *Reading the Old Testament: An Introduction*, (New York: The Paulist Press, 1984), p. 479.

or thrusting bayonets, in the service and for the selfish purposes of a master, such war degrades a people."[194] The reproductive rights debate is a metaphorical war between values: in this case, between life and reproductive rights. Norma L. McCorvey was used as a human instrument by a lawyer, Sarah Weddington, in the case that resulted in the Supreme Court ruling, called Roe versus Wade of 1973.[195] McCorvey was the "Roe" in Roe versus Wade, a pseudonym for Norma McCorvey. While she was under a lot of pressure to have one at the time, McCorvey never had an abortion, and today is a staunch opponent of Roe versus Wade in particular, and abortion in general. Yet, as we see in emotional political discourse, reproductive rights, as a meme, has shaped a dominating cultural view for many in our society.

Old Gadfly: IM, why are there no similar discussions in the public narrative?

IM: The current discussion is dominated by a progressive viewpoint. As I already mentioned, at one time earlier in my life, the first news source I read each morning was the *New York Times*. In those days, the *Times* newspaper was *the* bellwether news source. Other news outlets keyed off the *Times*. Today, the *Times* reporting and editorials reflect a political lens through which it observes and reports the news. Just this week, in an effort to rally behind the progressive presidential candidate, the paper published an editorial, "If Roe v. Wade Goes."[196] Citing progressive think tanks, the editorial was a blatant attempt to frighten women into thinking Romney and Ryan would advance policy to make abortion illegal, making abortion dangerous for those seeking one. Romney and Ryan believe abortion rights are something to be decided by the people within their respective states. But, progressives have a different view because they believe in a large central government with a statist perspective and moral superiority in "the authoritative allocation of values." In the process, those who dominate the public narrative propagate the memes that shape American culture.

Old Gadfly: IM, let me reinforce what you just described with thoughts from Walter Cronkite. Cronkite wrote the Preface to a 1983 edition of George Orwell's dystopian novel, *1984*. [197] Cronkite commended Orwell for the abundance and power of the symbols that capture the

---

[194] Mill, op cit.

[195] Sarah Weddington, *A Question of Choice*, (New York, NY: G. P. Putnam's Sons, 1992

[196] If Roe v Wade Goes," The New York Times, October 15, 2012. Available at http://www.nytimes.com/ 2012/10/16/opinion/if-roe-v-wade-goes.html?_r=0

[197] George Orwell, *1984,* (New York: Signet Classic, 1983), pp. 1-2.

tyranny of the time the book was originally published and the potential for such tyranny to appear in future ages. Cronkite then reminded us that we had met Big Brother: Stalin, Hitler, and Khomeini as obvious examples. Cronkite even claimed we hear "Newspeak" in our own public narratives.[198] Cronkite finally cautioned readers that if *1984* was not prophecy, it was most certainly a warning. The warning is about the threat to human freedom in a political environment that can combine organization and technology to create power on a scale unimaginable in previous generations.

IM: This was Cronkite in 1983! I would love to hear what he thinks about Obama's grassroots organizing effort in combination with today's social network communication technology.

Old Gadfly: The challenge for Americans who maintain a capacity to reason, IM, is to sufficiently educate other members of our society with the intellectual capacity and sense of discernment to (a) identify those memes that either arm politicians for abusive power or inspire politicians for character-based leadership; and (b) make informed decisions at the ballot box. The future of our individual freedom and the future of the American idea are at stake.

---

[198] George Lakoff demonstrates "Newspeak" in *Moral Politics: How Liberals and Conservatives Think* when he metaphorically classifies liberals as nurturing parents and conservatives as strict fathers.

10 TAKERS ARE PATHETIC FOOLS

November 14, 2012
Serrano's Coffee, Monument, Colorado

Old Gadfly: IM, have you recovered from the Presidential election?

IM: I'm still experiencing the grieving process. It's amazing. At first, I was raving mad. Then, I had doubt about my own assessment as to which candidate was best prepared to lead the nation. My doubts rapidly vanished yesterday when I discovered Obama's first step on the subject of our economy was to meet with union leaders, senior members of the Center for American Progress, and Moveon.org.[199]

Old Gadfly: Do you think those who voted for him realize what is happening?

IM: Do you mean like having a hangover after all the celebration?

Old Gadfly: My question was really rhetorical because I already know the answer.

IM: What do you mean?

Old Gadfly: There are two reasons why most of those who voted for Obama have no idea what is about to happen. First, most of them are Copernican drones that lack the capacity for discernment or independent research. Till now, they have not needed discernment because many of

---

[199] Amie Parnes and Niall Stanage, "'A Lot of Energy' in Obama's Meeting at White House with Liberal Groups," *The Hill.com*, November 13, 2012, available at http://thehill.com/homenews/administration/267737-a-lot-of-energy-in-obamas-meeting-at-white-house-with-liberal-groups

them have no desire to create or produce for the benefit of others. I know this sounds harsh; but, there are too many Americans who have grown complacent and dependent upon government subsidies. This lack of desire to create or produce for the benefit of others reflects the second reason: these creatures are takers.

IM: Gadfly, you do not sugar coat arguments. What do you think is about to happen?

Old Gadfly: The takers will multiply and this growing population will take more from the shrinking population of those who produce. Today, I heard Obama wants to raise $1.6 trillion in new revenue. He thinks he can do this by simply raising taxes on the wealthy. Those who produce will stop producing. There will be fewer jobs and less revenue. Chaos will emerge. Martial law can likely be imposed, and America will become a totalitarian state. Sounds absurd doesn't it?

IM: Yes.

Old Gadfly: Think about it. Obama has not met with small business leaders to ask them how the federal government can help them grow their businesses and create jobs. Not surprisingly, Obama's first step was to meet with union leaders who take profits from company owners for their indentured, dues paying takers. Indentured takers then owe their allegiance to the union leader that serves as a parasite, feeding off the wealth of its host, the wealth creator. Government unions are worse. Public servants are supposed to serve the public, not union leaders. Union leaders and union members are Obama's lieutenants and pit bulls that threaten and coerce the producers, just as George Orwell described in *Animal Farm* and Ayn Rand described in *Atlas Shrugged*.

IM: So, how does the Center for American Progress play into this scheme?

Old Gadfly: As we discussed in a previous conversation, the Center is the epicenter for creating the progressive message. The Center does not simply offer a set of beliefs. It teaches orthodoxy that is like a religious mandate for its followers. Remember, George Lakoff, in his book *Moral Politics: How Liberals and Conservatives Think*, explains that conservative values are not only wrong, they are immoral.

IM: Is the Center for American Progress a taker?

Old Gadfly: The Center provides the justification for taking from others in the form of entitlements controlled by a large, central, statist government. This taking is justified as social justice, so that the takers look like the givers to a growing number of takers.

IM: How about Moveon.org?

Old Gadfly: Moveon.org was founded and heavily funded by George Soros. Moveon.org is a means for communicating the progressive message.

IM: Obama has assembled a team for supposedly restoring our stagnant economy.

Old Gadfly: Yes, and this is why those who voted for Obama are not only takers, they are pathetic fools. They want more from others and will soon have less. Proverbs talks about such people who have existed for ages: dogs return to vomit, and fools return to folly (Proverbs 26:11). And the ultimate taker and fool is Obama, the person to which American takers have hitched their wagon—but all of us, to include those who have the capacity to discern and did not vote for Obama--will suffer the same misery if left unchallenged and uncorrected.

IM: The collapse of our nation sounds inevitable.

Old Gadfly: I'm not so certain about that. I'll tell you why. When convincing the British government not to intervene in the American Civil War, despite the nation's critical dependence upon cotton from the Southern states, John Stuart Mill observed:

War is an ugly thing, but not the ugliest of things: the decayed and degraded state of moral and patriotic feeling which thinks nothing worth a war, is worse. When a people are used as mere human instruments for firing cannon or thrusting bayonets, in the service and for the selfish purposes of a master, such war degrades a people. A war to protect other human beings against tyrannical injustice; a war to give victory to their own ideas of right and good, and which is their own war, carried on for an honest purpose by their free choice—is often the means of their regeneration. A man who has nothing which he is willing to fight for, nothing which he cares more about than he does about his personal safety, is a miserable creature, who has no chance of being free, unless made and kept so by the exertions of better men than himself. As long as justice and injustice have not terminated *their* ever renewing fight for ascendancy in the affairs of mankind, human beings must be willing, when need is, to do battle for the one against the other.[200]

---

[200] Mill, op cit.

IM: Gadfly, are you saying we are at war?

Old Gadfly: Absolutely. We **are** at war. Our war is between the indenturing orthodoxy of secular progressivism versus the liberating orthodoxy of Judeo-Christianity. Free men and women, who already create and produce for others, must continue to fight on the side of justice. Justice is fairness for everyone, not just for the protected classes determined by governing elite. These freedom and justice fighters obviously want safety and security for everyone. But more importantly, they will fight for the conditions that allow any person who so desires, to become self-actualized, not state-kept.

IM: Didn't Mill also write about liberty?

Old Gadfly: Yes, and one of the critical points Mill made in this work was that the true essence of liberty could only be attained if the people of a society are educated. Education involves the capacity to critically think, to discern. So, liberty is at risk in America, as the recent election demonstrated, because our current values-based education system has produced nearly three generations of Americans who lack this capacity (millions of Copernican drones) . . . for now. C. S. Lewis cautioned us about these developments in his book, *The Abolition of Man*, and F. A. Hayek addressed the danger of politically correct values in the Chapter, "The End of Truth" in his book, *The Road to Serfdom*.

IM: It seems as though we have an educational and political movement in America that actually encourages taking.

Old Gadfly: Good point, IM. I think we can conclude from our discussion that there are two levels of takers in America: political elite who take from others as an egalitarian step toward social justice and equality, and those who take subsidies for little to nothing in return. While the latter are what Mill would call miserable creatures, both are pathetic fools because they attempt to perpetuate a system that is unsustainable. Having said this, there are many who need help. When our nation was founded, there was an appreciation for the role institutions play in this regard.

IM: What do you mean by institutions?

Old Gadfly: By institutions I refer to a range of entities that are based on rules or norms that shape orderly and constructive behavior within a society or regimes within a society. Institutions range from government to corporations, churches, neighborhoods, associations, and so forth. There are many ways to help people in need and a society that appreciates and respects the value of these diverse institutions is more likely to promote the unalienable individual rights of life, liberty, and the pursuit of happiness.

IM: So, how do we reverse the current educational and political movement that promotes taking?

Old Gadfly: In broad terms, we must provide a clear and compelling alternative that focuses on balancing individual liberty (and the expectations of being a responsible American citizen) with the need for a diverse set of institutions that bring novelty and opportunity in advancing human progress, not simply sustaining safety and security. We must also make very clear how the progressive ideology depends upon Mill's notion of human instruments. Perhaps in future discussions we will have the opportunity to further develop these ideas.

11 POLITICAL PROSTITUTION

November 21, 2012
O'Malley's Pub & Grill, Palmer Lake, Colorado

Old Gadfly: IM, do you remember the Rush Limbaugh controversy about calling Sandra Fluke a prostitute?

IM: Yes, I remember. Even President Obama got involved by calling Fluke to offer support and harshly criticized Limbaugh for the comment.

Old Gadfly: Why did Limbaugh risk such criticism?

IM: He did not like the fact that Fluke wanted free contraception, and because she became a symbolic wedge in the debate between a government mandate and the Catholic Church's insistence upon freedom of religion. In this case, the Catholic Church, which serves as an employer and self-insures, did not want to be coerced into paying for contraception because the mandate violates one of the Church's doctrines.

Old Gadfly: Fluke is not married. So, why does she want contraception?

IM: A prudish comment, Gadfly. Fluke wants to be protected from unwanted pregnancies. Except for artificial insemination, a woman can only become pregnant from sexual activity with a man. So, does this not make Fluke a prostitute?

Old Gadfly: Technically no. A prostitute, or equivalent term such as whore, harlot, or strumpet, solicits and accepts payment for sex. There is no indication Fluke has done this.

IM: Hearing you say words like whore, harlot, and strumpet seems harsh, Gadfly.

Old Gadfly: IM, alcoholics do not have the exclusive claim on a life of denial. Other behaviors that take on a force of habit also suffer denial, such as gluttony, envy, pride, sloth, greed, and so forth.

IM: You just listed what the Christian religion refers to as capital sins.

Old Gadfly: Very true. And while Sandra Fluke may not be a prostitute, more accurate terms to describe her behavior include promiscuous, licentious, wanton, unchaste, lecherous, and lascivious. These behaviors stem from lust, another capital sin.

IM: But, these so called capital sins really only make sense from a religious perspective.

Old Gadfly: Yes, but how about secular progressive capital sins that violate political correctness such as racism, homophobia, doubts about causes of global warming, pro-life views that challenge claims of reproductive rights, and so forth? These examples are equivalent to capital sins from a secular progressive worldview.

IM: Good point. So, why did Fluke speak at the Democratic National Convention?

Old Gadfly: Of course, Fluke was invited by Obama's team for engineering public sentiment. Her presence and speech at the Democratic National Convention was designed to symbolize and rally many single women who subscribe to her view of life, want free contraception, and thus voted for Obama because of his strident position in favor of and encouragement of this kind of behavior.

IM: I see what you mean, Gadfly; but, this conversation still makes me very uncomfortable because these explicit conversations rarely occur nowadays.

Old Gadfly: By the way, recall in our last conversation, we included John Stuart Mill's observation about people being "used as mere human instruments for firing cannon or thrusting bayonets, in the service and for the selfish purposes of a master."[201] Obama's "engineering public sentiment" team obviously used Sandra Fluke as an instrument in the Presidential election contest.

IM: It seems that way.

Old Gadfly: So, how about Sister Simone Campbell, Executive Director of Network and leader of the Nuns on a Bus project, who, in addition to Sandra Fluke, also spoke at the Democratic National Convention?

IM: I remember watching her speech when she criticized the Romney-Ryan plan that would hurt the poor, citing the United States Conference of Catholic Bishops who claimed the Ryan budget failed a basic moral test because it would harm families currently in poverty.

---

[201] Mill, op cit.

Old Gadfly: Yes, Sister Campbell and the Bishops criticized a plan that has yet to be implemented. The Ryan plan at this point was more theory than evidence.

IM: Where are you headed with this point?

Old Gadfly: Sister Campbell obviously endorsed Obama and, by implication, all of his policies. How have Obama's policies benefited the poor over the past four years?

IM: The number of families on food stamps has significantly increased. Median annual incomes have decreased by more than $4,000 for the middle class. The percentage of those families below the poverty level has also increased. And, since the end of his predecessor's term, and despite claims of "creating over 5 million jobs," Obama's policies have actually resulted in net job losses of over 2 million, and a significantly lower labor force participation rate, from 65.8% in December 2008 to 63.8% at the end of October 2012.

Old Gadfly: IM, you just described actual evidence that strongly suggests Obama's policies are actually hurting the poor and the middle class, not helping them.

IM: So, why would Sister Campbell bet on Obama's losing track record over an untested plan that is designed to strengthen the economy with new jobs and corresponding increases in the quality of life for everyone, which seems very progressive, that is, actual progress for humankind?

Old Gadfly: Clever thought about the ideal meaning of progressivism. You know, the political progressive movement, which drives the Democratic Party's current vision, employs social justice as the means of achieving equal outcomes for the masses, which has little to do with progress. But, back to Sister Campbell . . . What is even more ironic, how could Sister Campbell back a candidate who believes nearly half a billion of federal funding per year is not enough to support Planned Parenthood and its major abortion industry, which stems from the progressive movement's doctrine that protects a woman's reproductive right?

IM: Now I see where you were heading on this point. Sister Campbell was looking for something, perhaps prestige, branding, or financial grants, in return for her public support, thus prostituting her Catholic affiliation for political gain.

Old Gadfly: Yes. This behavior made me realize there is a profound difference between a progressive Catholic and a Catholic progressive. A progressive Catholic modifies her religious positions based on her political views--in this case, the secular progressive doctrine of social justice, where political elite establish rights and provide for the masses. On the other hand, a Catholic progressive modifies her political positions based on her religious views--in this case, the Catholic doctrine of natural law and respect for life. This dichotomy may explain why 50% of Catholic voters voted for Obama and 48% for Romney. Progressive Catholics now seem to outnumber Catholic progressives.

IM: The subtle, yet profound distinction between progressive Catholics and Catholic progressives has powerful implications, Gadfly. For starters, the Old Testament documents similar struggles between secularism and religion during the cultural evolution of the Jewish community more than two thousand years ago.

Old Gadfly: Excellent point to wrap up our discussion, IM. I look forward to discussing the implications of the American cultural evolution associated with progressivism in greater depth with you.

12 HONEYMOON TONIGHT, MARRIAGE TOMORROW?

November 29, 2012
The Coffee Cup Café, Monument, Colorado

Old Gadfly: IM, in my younger, single days I once heard a man ask a woman to start a honeymoon that evening with the promise he would marry her the next day. What do you think he was doing?

IM: Obviously, the man was enticing the woman to meet his personal desire with a promise that he would marry her after his desire was met. Promises are not always kept; but, worse, some abusive marriages (especially those that spinoff from such a spontaneous encounter, without the benefit of a more traditional courtship) are difficult to dissolve.

Old Gadfly: Exactly, IM. Do you see analogous behaviors playing out in American political affairs?

IM: Yes. Although, I must admit, Obama enticed the American public to elect him, twice, with a promise of hope and change. The reelection does make me think about the battered women syndrome.

Old Gadfly: Let's discuss specific details, such as promises kept and not kept, the nature of the current marriage Obama has with the American people, and the consequences of no traditional courtship and the battered women syndrome.

IM: I'll start with promises kept.

- First, Obama promised change. Now, I must admit when talking to younger people who enthusiastically campaigned for him, none, not one, could tell me what change meant. I just wanted one example, such as major reform of the healthcare system, major reform of the tax system, or bipartisanship in Washington

D.C. These examples were what I inferred from his campaign speeches. But these young people didn't care about details. What I got in return was a glassy-eyed blind allegiance to a man they hardly knew. But, as we know, Obama did bring change. He did win landmark major healthcare legislation without a single Republican vote. Yet, for such a self-proclaimed historical achievement, the legislation involved stealing over 700 billion from Medicare accounts and we continue to hear about waivers for special interest groups and how businesses are laying off employees because of the increased costs of providing healthcare. My own insurance premiums have already risen and as I approach the age of 65, I see fewer and fewer care providers accepting Medicare patients.

- Second, Obama promised to wind down military operations in Iraq and to shift the military effort to Afghanistan, where the real focus should be. The Iraq withdrawal timeline had already been established by his predecessor, pending conditions within the region. Obama kept to the timeline, despite failing to establish a Status of Forces Agreement with the Iraqi government. Now, Iraq is at risk with pressures from Iran and Syria. In Afghanistan, Obama did increase forces, but well-below what was requested. Now, Obama is seeking to withdraw from an intractable situation. So, Obama kept his promises, with himself as the only winner, and many losers, in the outcome.

Old Gadfly: IM, are the American people so naïve that they do not understand the implications of what you just described?

IM: Naïve seems like a good description, but in keeping with the theme of our conversation, I would suggest the battered women syndrome is a more accurate characterization. I'll expand on this notion later. For now, let me talk about promises not kept.

- First, Obama promised to cut deficits in half by the end of his first term.
  - o The worst annual deficit during his predecessor's eight years in office was less than $500 billion. Every year of the past four years had deficits well in excess of $1 trillion. Yes, the Bush era deficits contributed $4 trillion to the national debt over the eight-year term. But, Obama contributed between $5 and $6 trillion in only four years. So, it seems the honeymoon bliss dominates any marital obligations.
  - o Ironically, I was leafing through one of the textbooks you use when teaching ethics to your students. I noticed a quote from U.S. District Judge Leonard Sand when sentencing John and Timothy Rigas for fraudulently looting $100

million from Adelphia Communications.[202] He criticized the defendants for spending other people's money. John Rigas founded the company in 1952. Fifty-three years later, after creating thousands of jobs and billions in wealth for stockholders and stakeholders, his company faced bankruptcy with $2.5 billion in debt. Although John was 80 at the time, and suffering from bladder cancer, the judge sentenced him to 15 years in prison.[203] Now, let me provide some context.

- Solyndra, a California-based green energy company, received a $535 million government loan with strong backing from President Obama.[204] Less than a year later, the company declared bankruptcy. Based on the language in the loan, the U.S. government ended up writing off the entire amount. But, bonuses were honored. The $535 million came from taxpayers. Other people spent their money on a risky and failed investment. No one was prosecuted.

- Even more egregious, the financial crisis of 2008 stemmed from the housing bubble. As one of our previous conversations revealed, Fannie Mae and Freddie Mac were primarily responsible for generating the subprime mortgages that led to creative financial maneuvering by the financial sector mandated by Congress to purchase the toxic assets. Combined, these government supported enterprises cost the American taxpayers $274 billion in bailout funds.[205] Between 2008 and now, bonuses have been paid at taxpayer expense. Again, not a single person was prosecuted.

---

[202] Marianne M. Jennings, Business Ethics: Case Studies and Selected Readings, (Mason, OH: South-Western Cengage Learning, 2012), p. 189.

[203] Patricia Hurtado, "John Rigas Gets 15 Years, Son 20," The Baltimore Sun, June 21, 2005. Retrieved from http://articles.baltimoresun.com/2005-06-21/business/0506210262_1_john-rigas-adelphia-communications-sentencing

[204] Rachel Weiner, "Solyndra, Explained," *The Washington Post*, June 1, 2012. Retrieved from http://www.washingtonpost.com/blogs/the-fix/post/solyndra--explained/2012/06/01/gJQAig2g6U_blog.html

[205] Rachelle Younglai, "U.S. Tightens Reins on Fannie Mae, Freddie Mac," Reuters, August 17, 2012. Retrieved from http://www.reuters.com/article/2012/08/17/us-usa-housing-idUSBRE87G0EN20120817

- ▪ I wonder if John Rigas would have received more mercy had he claimed the government built his business.
- A second Obama promise included reducing unemployment to 6% by the end of his first term. As we know, it still hovers around 8%.
  - o Instead of thanking the top 1% or 2% for paying 60-70% of the tax revenue, Obama demonizes this group for not "paying its fair share" even though they do not get a fair share in terms of government services or voting privileges. Whether one pays a million dollars in taxes or none, each still gets one vote.
  - o Yet, for a clever politician who claims to want to improve financial conditions for the middle and lower classes, one would think he might be open to learning how wealth creation actually takes place in a relatively free society. He demonizes the one segment of our society that can actually unleash trillions of reserve capital into the type of investment that generates new jobs and more wealth.
  - o The only jobs governments create are government jobs, which create no wealth and are a further drain on an economy. Obama campaigned on making the wealthy pay their fair share while cutting federal spending. This is the honeymoon appeal. As we know there are no budget cuts. This is the promise of marriage tomorrow.
- A third Obama promise was to lead the most transparent Administration in the history of our Nation. Of course, we all know the expectation for transparency is accountability to the American public.
  - o When Congress pushed for additional documentation related to the Fast & Furious Operation, President Obama declared the documents were protected by executive privilege. This declaration meant one of two realities: (a) Obama did in fact have personal knowledge about the operation when he had publicly claimed no knowledge, or (b) he abused the power of executive privilege to block full disclosure to Congress.
  - o As we know, another transparency issue continues to play out regarding the events in Benghazi, Libya prior to the election. Secretary of State Hillary Clinton at least "accepted responsibility" for the fatalities. That's noble; yet, there is no accountability. Perhaps, Michael Moore can build on an old Bush cliché. "Bush lied and people died" has morphed into "people died and Obama (and Rice, and Clinton, and Clapper) lied."

o There are certainly many other issues related to transparency, but I must confess that I believe what Obama means by transparency is that he will assertively tell the American public what Obama or his strategic communication advisors (i.e., David Axelrod, David Plouffe, Anita Dunn, and Robert Gibbs) determine the public **needs** to know, whether it's a manufactured picture through plausible spin or actual reality.[206] The key to Obama's success is telling the right story; he even admitted this during a CBS News interview with Charlie Rose.[207] This may explain why he has spent the majority of his time traveling to various parts of the country in "campaign mode." Tell people what they want to hear--hope is on the way. These behaviors represent the abusive part of the battered wife syndrome, where control is so important.

Old Gadfly: IM, I see the connection to honeymoon and marriage, but I do not grasp the connection to the battered women syndrome.

IM: This one is more complicated. According to the American Judges Association, there are at least three characteristics of the battered women syndrome.[208]

- The first characteristic is the fight mode. "The body and mind prepare to deal with danger by becoming hyper-vigilant to cues of potential violence, resulting in an exaggerated startle response." Obama has achieved this result by manufacturing threats against sexual orientation, reproductive rights, and civil rights for undocumented immigrants, and so forth.

- The second characteristic is the flight response. "When physical escape is actually, or perceived as, impossible, then mental escape occurs. This is the avoidance or emotional numbing stage where denial, minimization, rationalization and disassociation are subconsciously used as ways to psychologically escape from the threat or presence of violence." Obama capitalized on this by

---

[206] For evidence see the YouTube video of Anita Dunn explaining this approach at http://www.youtube.com/ watch?v=NlGNhAnwp_Y

[207] Lindsey Boerma, "Obama Reflects on His Biggest Mistake as President," CBS News, July 12, 2012. Available at http://www.cbsnews.com/8301-503544_162-57471351-503544/obama-reflects-on-his-biggest-mistake-as-president/

[208] "Domestic Violence & the Courtroom: Knowing the Issues . . . Understanding the Victim," American Judges Association, no date. Available at http://aja.ncsc.dni.us/pdfs/domestic-violence-the-courtroom.pdf

emphasizing fears for the first characteristic. This kept people from focusing on domestic economic and foreign policy failures.

- The third characteristic is cognitive ability and memory loss:

  Here, the victim begins to have intrusive memories of the abuse or may actually develop psychogenic amnesia and not always remember important details or events. The victim may have trouble following his or her thoughts in a logical way, being distracted by intrusive memories that may be flashbacks to previous battering incidents. The victim may disassociate himself or herself when faced with painful events, memories, reoccurring nightmares or other associations not readily apparent to the observer.[209]

This is why human instruments like Sandra Fluke and Sister Simone Campbell were so effective at the Democratic National Convention.

- o Fluke reminded single women of how Republicans threatened their reproductive rights and entitlement to free contraceptives or abortifacients.
- o Sister Campbell let the middle and lower class know the Romney-Ryan economic plan would further jeopardize their financial well-being.

- As the American Judges Association understands from psychiatric evidence, perception control is an important feature in a battered women syndrome relationship. Guilt is one manifestation.[210] Consequently, for any American that might feel he or she is being abused by Obama, the fact that he is black conjures up fears and guilt of being accused of being a racist or bigot.

Old Gadfly: You are correct about the analogy of the battered women syndrome being complicated. But, your explanation certainly makes sense. At the beginning of our conversation, you mentioned traditional courtship. What are your thoughts along these lines?

IM: In my lifetime, the traditional courtship with presidential candidates involved a fairly objective vetting by a free press. Of course, there is plenty of evidence that the media has always displayed a political bias throughout history. But I must admit that during my lifetime, I have not witnessed such a lopsided display of bias; and, thus, the dismissal of any

---

[209] Ibid.

[210] Ibid.

such need for a courtship.

Old Gadfly: Why do you think this happened?

IM: My theory is that we are experiencing an intellectual hubris that has thoroughly penetrated the media, government, and academia since around the 1960s. People that migrate to these three regimes tend to pride themselves as being members of the "educated class" with a moral obligation to govern the "underclass." Of course, the conditions that provided fertility for this movement started in the early 20th Century with an intellectual fascination and love affair with (a) socialism, as a political economic philosophy; and (b) statism, as an effective way of governing a society. Woodrow Wilson and Franklin Delano Roosevelt, empowered by large democratic majorities in both houses of Congress, pushed aggressively to change institutions of government based on principles of socialism and statism. Given the public malaise and discontent of the 1960s, characterized by hippies, drugs, and an unpopular Vietnam conflict, one of the triggering mechanisms for accelerating this movement was the Port Huron Statement of the Students for a Democratic Society, primarily authored by John Hayden, a University of Michigan student and later and elected official and husband to Jane Fonda.[211] In a sense, this document embodied the emotions and passions of a college-age generation, and represented a new Declaration of Independence to liberate a new generation from the perceived oppression of accumulated traditions that characterized America in the early 1960s.

In arguing for an activist agenda, the Statement claimed "A new left must include liberals and socialists, the former for their relevance, the latter for their sense of thoroughgoing reforms in the system. The university is a more sensible place than a political party for these two traditions to begin to discuss their differences and look for political synthesis."[212] This likely explains why 85% or more university faculty today are registered Democrats. Yet, what this 1962 declaration missed in history is that it was a new left that allowed Hitler to achieve political power in the 1930s. As Hayek, quoting extensively from German scholars, explained in *The Road to Serfdom*, the contest between liberal and socialistic perspectives reached a tipping point, which resulted in fascism.

Old Gadfly: Wait a minute, IM. It is commonly accepted that fascism was a far right manifestation.

IM: I know, Gadfly. Most people believe communism is the far

---

[211] "Port Huron Statement of the Students for a Democratic Society, 1962,"
Courtesy Office of Senator Tom Hayden. Available at
http://coursesa.matrix.msu.edu/~hst306/documents/huron.html

[212] Ibid.

left equivalent of a far right fascism. This cannot be further from the truth. Think about it. As conservative ideology moves from center to right the ideology becomes increasingly libertarian, with an increasing emphasis on limited and smaller government. At its most extreme, this ideology would result in anarchy. As liberal ideology moves from center to left it becomes more progressive and socialistic, in anticipation of an inevitable transition to communism and an increasing emphasis on a larger and more centralized government. In Germany and Italy, the political center moved progressively left. And, when socialism did not sustain the needs of the masses, instead of the emergence of communism, the states devolved into fascism. For an excellent background on the actual roots of fascism, read Chapter Two, "The Great Utopia," in Hayek's *The Road to Serfdom*.

Old Gadfly: This explanation will not convince a lot of people who believe otherwise.

IM: This is true, Gadfly. Unfortunately, a consequence of the critical theory and postmodern philosophy that so impressed college students in the 60s and inspired the Port Huron Statement is a distortion of truth. These activists truly believed then and believe now that truth is created, not discovered. We live in a world now where formerly accepted truth is heresy, and an imagined utopia becomes truth.

Old Gadfly: About the time of the Port Huron Statement, I recall a speech by retired Admiral Ben Moreell. The speech made an impression on me because Moreell delivered it on the same day John F. Kennedy was assassinated, November 22, 1963. The title of his speech was "The Right to Be Wrong."[213] Moreell argued against the push to centralize more power in Washington. He provided evidence of an increasing preference for egalitarian policies in the name of social justice at the expense of individual rights. The push was disguised as "democracy" when in fact it was "socialism." Moreell cautioned that we should heed the warning of Dean William Ralph Inge who observed that throughout history, the greatest triumphs of the powers of evil consist of capturing or coopting organizations designed to defeat them; once captured or coopted, and the devil has altered the contents, he preserves the original labels. In other words, he has changed the essence of the original concept or truth.[214]

IM: Excellent point, Gadfly. So, as we wrap up our conversation, I am still taken aback that Obama and the Democrats in Congress believe the Republicans will buy the honeymoon tonight for marriage tomorrow

---

[213] Admiral Ben Moreell, "The Right to Be Wrong," *Vital Speeches of the Day*, Vol. 30, No. 5, December 15, 1963.

[214] W. R. Inge, *Christian Ethics & Modern Problems (1930)*, (New York, NY: G. P. Putnam's Sons, 1930), p. 142.

proposition. They truly believe the Republicans will accept tax hikes today for a promise of budget cuts in the future. What is really insulting is that when Democrats call for compromise, they really mean Republican capitulation. And, not surprising, the public will read about the mainstream media's claim of Republican obstructionism.

13 CONCLUSIONS AND IMPLICATIONS

December 31, 2012
O'Malley's Pub & Grill, Palmer Lake, Colorado

Old Gadfly: IM, since August, we have had a number of conversations about the American political contest. As we bring this year to a close, do you have any conclusions based on our conversations?

IM: Yes. I have two major conclusions. First, Americans appear to becoming less aware and discerning about the world in which they live. This I believe is a byproduct of educational and political reforms that are progressive. I know we used the word "progressive" frequently in our discussions. Yet, I believe many who call themselves "progressive" do not truly understand what that concept means politically and why the progressive ideology is dangerous. The implication is that I believe we should find a way to expose the progressive movement to those who are still aware and discerning of the world in which we live.

Old Gadfly: I agree, IM. Let's engage in some conversations about the progressive ideology in the coming year. Ideally, we might find a way to reach out to as many Americans as we can about this movement. What is your second major conclusion?

IM: My second conclusion is that while many Americans are becoming less aware and discerning about the world in which they live, many of those who have the capacity for awareness and discernment lack the character to be responsible citizens and leaders. I say this because, as we discussed in many of our conversations, there is far too much evidence of complicity, duplicity, and mendacity in public and private affairs. As a consequence, our nation steadily marches toward a fiscal and spiritual cliff. Some deliberately deceive to gain or keep power; others go along to get along. The implication is that we must find a way to re-instill traditional spiritual and political values associated with virtue.

Old Gadfly: So, I hear you saying we can learn much from human affairs in history.

IM: Yes. I strongly believe the only concept that separates modernity from antiquity in terms of human affairs is technology. Technology brings benefits and consequences. As we discussed earlier, Neil Postman in his book, *Amusing Ourselves to Death*, provided solid analysis and prophecy along these lines. The fundamental issues related to human intercourse throughout history have not changed. Humans tend to orient toward conflict or cooperation.

Old Gadfly: Another excellent conclusion and description of its implication, IM. Incidentally, I am currently drafting a manuscript on the art of peace. It will address your second conclusion and corresponding implication. I look forward to discussing the various subthemes with you.

IM: Meanwhile, let's enjoy New Year's Eve with great anticipation for meaningful and constructive hope and change in 2013.

Old Gadfly: Thank you for the enlightening conversations. Be safe; see you next year.

APPENDIX A: TRANSCRIPT OF REMARKS BY PRESIDENT OBAMA ON FISCAL POLICY

The White House[215]
Office of the Press Secretary
For Immediate Release
April 13, 2011
George Washington University
Washington, D.C.
1:48 P.M. EDT
THE PRESIDENT: Thank you very much. (Applause.) Please have a seat. Please have a seat, everyone.

It is wonderful to be back at GW. I want you to know that one of the reasons that I worked so hard with Democrats and Republicans to keep the government open was so that I could show up here today. I wanted to make sure that all of you had one more excuse to skip class. (Laughter.) You're welcome. (Laughter.)

I want to give a special thanks to Steven Knapp, the president of GW. I just saw him -- where is he? There he is right there. (Applause.)

We've got a lot of distinguished guests here -- a couple of people I want to acknowledge. First of all, my outstanding Vice President, Joe Biden, is here. (Applause.) Our Secretary of the Treasury, Tim Geithner, is in the house. (Applause.) Jack Lew, the Director of the Office of Management and Budget. (Applause.) Gene Sperling, Chair of the National Economic Council, is here. (Applause.) Members of our bipartisan Fiscal Commission

---

[215] Remarks by the President were retrieved from
http://www.whitehouse.gov/the-press-office/2011/04/13/remarks-president-fiscal-policy

are here, including the two outstanding chairs -- Erskine Bowles and Alan Simpson -- are here. (Applause.)

And we have a number of members of Congress here today. I'm grateful for all of you taking the time to attend.

What we've been debating here in Washington over the last few weeks will affect the lives of the students here and families all across America in potentially profound ways. This debate over budgets and deficits is about more than just numbers on a page; it's about more than just cutting and spending. It's about the kind of future that we want. It's about the kind of country that we believe in. And that's what I want to spend some time talking about today.

From our first days as a nation, we have put our faith in free markets and free enterprise as the engine of America's wealth and prosperity. More than citizens of any other country, we are rugged individualists, a self-reliant people with a healthy skepticism of too much government.

But there's always been another thread running through our history -- a belief that we're all connected, and that there are some things we can only do together, as a nation. We believe, in the words of our first Republican President, Abraham Lincoln, that through government, we should do together what we cannot do as well for ourselves.

And so we've built a strong military to keep us secure, and public schools and universities to educate our citizens. We've laid down railroads and highways to facilitate travel and commerce. We've supported the work of scientists and researchers whose discoveries have saved lives, unleashed repeated technological revolutions, and led to countless new jobs and entire new industries. Each of us has benefitted from these investments, and we're a more prosperous country as a result.

Part of this American belief that we're all connected also expresses itself in a conviction that each one of us deserves some basic measure of security and dignity. We recognize that no matter how responsibly we live our lives, hard times or bad luck, a crippling illness or a layoff may strike any one of us. "There but for the grace of God go I," we say to ourselves. And so we contribute to programs like Medicare and Social Security, which guarantee us health care and a measure of basic income after a lifetime of hard work; unemployment insurance, which protects us against unexpected job loss; and Medicaid, which provides care for millions of seniors in nursing homes, poor children, those with disabilities. We're a better country because of these commitments. I'll go further. We would not be a great country without those commitments.

Now, for much of the last century, our nation found a way to afford these investments and priorities with the taxes paid by its citizens. As a country that values fairness, wealthier individuals have traditionally borne a greater share of this burden than the middle class or those less fortunate. Everybody pays, but the wealthier have borne a little more. This is not because we begrudge those who've done well -- we rightly celebrate their success. Instead, it's a basic reflection of our belief that those who've benefited most from our way of life can afford to give back a little bit more. Moreover, this belief hasn't hindered the success of those at the top of the income scale. They continue to do better and better with each passing year.

Now, at certain times -- particularly during war or recession -- our nation has had to borrow money to pay for some of our priorities. And as most families understand, a little credit card debt isn't going to hurt if it's temporary.

But as far back as the 1980s, America started amassing debt at more alarming levels, and our leaders began to realize that a larger challenge was on the horizon. They knew that eventually, the Baby Boom generation would retire, which meant a much bigger portion of our citizens would be relying on programs like Medicare, Social Security, and possibly Medicaid. Like parents with young children who know they have to start saving for the college years, America had to start borrowing less and saving more to prepare for the retirement of an entire generation.

To meet this challenge, our leaders came together three times during the 1990s to reduce our nation's deficit -- three times. They forged historic agreements that required tough decisions made by the first President Bush, then made by President Clinton, by Democratic Congresses and by a Republican Congress. All three agreements asked for shared responsibility and shared sacrifice. But they largely protected the middle class; they largely protected our commitment to seniors; they protected our key investments in our future.

As a result of these bipartisan efforts, America's finances were in great shape by the year 2000. We went from deficit to surplus. America was actually on track to becoming completely debt free, and we were prepared for the retirement of the Baby Boomers.

But after Democrats and Republicans committed to fiscal discipline during the 1990s, we lost our way in the decade that followed. We increased spending dramatically for two wars and an expensive prescription drug program -- but we didn't pay for any of this new spending. Instead, we made the problem worse with trillions of dollars in unpaid-for tax cuts -- tax cuts that went to every millionaire and billionaire in the country; tax cuts that will force us to borrow an average of $500 billion every year over the next decade.

To give you an idea of how much damage this caused to our nation's checkbook, consider this: In the last decade, if we had simply found a way to pay for the tax cuts and the prescription drug benefit, our deficit would currently be at low historical levels in the coming years.

But that's not what happened. And so, by the time I took office, we once again found ourselves deeply in debt and unprepared for a Baby Boom retirement that is now starting to take place. When I took office, our projected deficit, annually, was more than $1 trillion. On top of that, we faced a terrible financial crisis and a recession that, like most recessions, led us to temporarily borrow even more.

In this case, we took a series of emergency steps that saved millions of jobs, kept credit flowing, and provided working families extra money in their pocket. It was absolutely the right thing to do, but these steps were expensive, and added to our deficits in the short term.

So that's how our fiscal challenge was created. That's how we got here. And now that our economic recovery is gaining strength, Democrats and Republicans must come together and restore the fiscal responsibility that served us so well in the 1990s. We have to live within our means. We have to reduce our deficit, and we have to get back on a path that will allow us to pay down our debt. And we have to do it in a way that protects the recovery, protects the investments we need to grow, create jobs, and helps us win the future.

Now, before I get into how we can achieve this goal, some of you, particularly the younger people here -- you don't qualify, Joe. (Laughter.) Some of you might be wondering, "Why is this so important? Why does this matter to me?"

Well, here's why. Even after our economy recovers, our government will still be on track to spend more money than it takes in throughout this decade and beyond. That means we'll have to keep borrowing more from countries like China. That means more of your tax dollars each year will go towards paying off the interest on all the loans that we keep taking out. By the end of this decade, the interest that we owe on our debt could rise to nearly $1 trillion. Think about that. That's the interest -- just the interest payments.

Then, as the Baby Boomers start to retire in greater numbers and health care costs continue to rise, the situation will get even worse. By 2025, the amount of taxes we currently pay will only be enough to finance our health care programs -- Medicare and Medicaid -- Social Security, and the interest we owe on our debt. That's it. Every other national priority -- education, transportation, even our national security -- will have to be paid for with borrowed money.

Now, ultimately, all this rising debt will cost us jobs and damage our economy. It will prevent us from making the investments we need to win the future. We won't be able to afford good schools, new research, or the repair of roads -- all the things that create new jobs and businesses here in America. Businesses will be less likely to invest and open shop in a country that seems unwilling or unable to balance its books. And if our creditors start worrying that we may be unable to pay back our debts, that could drive up interest rates for everybody who borrows money -- making it harder for businesses to expand and hire, or families to take out a mortgage.

Here's the good news: That doesn't have to be our future. That doesn't have to be the country that we leave our children. We can solve this problem. We came together as Democrats and Republicans to meet this challenge before; we can do it again.

But that starts by being honest about what's causing our deficit. You see, most Americans tend to dislike government spending in the abstract, but like the stuff that it buys. Most of us, regardless of party affiliation, believe that we should have a strong military and a strong defense. Most Americans believe we should invest in education and medical research. Most Americans think we should protect commitments like Social Security and Medicare. And without even looking at a poll, my finely honed political instincts tell me that almost nobody believes they should be paying higher taxes. (Laughter.)

So because all this spending is popular with both Republicans and Democrats alike, and because nobody wants to pay higher taxes, politicians are often eager to feed the impression that solving the problem is just a matter of eliminating waste and abuse. You'll hear that phrase a lot. "We just need to eliminate waste and abuse." The implication is that tackling the deficit issue won't require tough choices. Or politicians suggest that we can somehow close our entire deficit by eliminating things like foreign aid, even though foreign aid makes up about 1 percent of our entire federal budget.

So here's the truth. Around two-thirds of our budget -- two-thirds -- is spent on Medicare, Medicaid, Social Security, and national security. Two-thirds. Programs like unemployment insurance, student loans, veterans' benefits, and tax credits for working families take up another 20 percent. What's left, after interest on the debt, is just 12 percent for everything else. That's 12 percent for all of our national priorities -- education, clean energy, medical research, transportation, our national parks, food safety, keeping our air and water clean -- you name it -- all of that accounts for 12 percent of our budget.

Now, up till now, the debate here in Washington, the cuts proposed by a lot of folks in Washington, have focused exclusively on that 12 percent. But cuts to that 12 percent alone won't solve the problem. So any serious plan to tackle our deficit will require us to put everything on the table, and take on excess spending wherever it exists in the budget.

A serious plan doesn't require us to balance our budget overnight -- in fact, economists think that with the economy just starting to grow again, we need a phased-in approach — but it does require tough decisions and support from our leaders in both parties now. Above all, it will require us to choose a vision of the America we want to see five years, 10 years, 20 years down the road.

Now, to their credit, one vision has been presented and championed by Republicans in the House of Representatives and embraced by several of their party's presidential candidates. It's a plan that aims to reduce our deficit by $4 trillion over the next 10 years, and one that addresses the challenge of Medicare and Medicaid in the years after that.

These are both worthy goals. They're worthy goals for us to achieve. But the way this plan achieves those goals would lead to a fundamentally different America than the one we've known certainly in my lifetime. In fact, I think it would be fundamentally different than what we've known throughout our history.

A 70 percent cut in clean energy. A 25 percent cut in education. A 30 percent cut in transportation. Cuts in college Pell Grants that will grow to more than $1,000 per year. That's the proposal. These aren't the kind of cuts you make when you're trying to get rid of some waste or find extra savings in the budget. These aren't the kinds of cuts that the Fiscal Commission proposed. These are the kinds of cuts that tell us we can't afford the America that I believe in and I think you believe in.

I believe it paints a vision of our future that is deeply pessimistic. It's a vision that says if our roads crumble and our bridges collapse, we can't afford to fix them. If there are bright young Americans who have the drive and the will but not the money to go to college, we can't afford to send them.

Go to China and you'll see businesses opening research labs and solar facilities. South Korean children are outpacing our kids in math and science. They're scrambling to figure out how they put more money into education. Brazil is investing billions in new infrastructure and can run half their cars not on high-priced gasoline, but on biofuels. And yet, we are presented with a vision that says the American people, the United States of America -- the greatest nation on Earth -- can't afford any of this.

It's a vision that says America can't afford to keep the promise we've made to care for our seniors. It says that 10 years from now, if you're a 65-year-old who's eligible for Medicare, you should have to pay nearly $6,400 more than you would today. It says instead of guaranteed health care, you will get a voucher. And if that voucher isn't worth enough to buy the insurance that's available in the open marketplace, well, tough luck -- you're on your own. Put simply, it ends Medicare as we know it.

It's a vision that says up to 50 million Americans have to lose their health insurance in order for us to reduce the deficit. Who are these 50 million Americans? Many are somebody's grandparents -- may be one of yours -- who wouldn't be able to afford nursing home care without Medicaid. Many are poor children. Some are middle-class families who have children with autism or Down's syndrome. Some of these kids with disabilities are -- the disabilities are so severe that they require 24-hour care. These are the Americans we'd be telling to fend for themselves.

And worst of all, this is a vision that says even though Americans can't afford to invest in education at current levels, or clean energy, even though we can't afford to maintain our commitment on Medicare and Medicaid, we can somehow afford more than $1 trillion in new tax breaks for the wealthy. Think about that.

In the last decade, the average income of the bottom 90 percent of all working Americans actually declined. Meanwhile, the top 1 percent saw their income rise by an average of more than a quarter of a million dollars each. That's who needs to pay less taxes?

They want to give people like me a $200,000 tax cut that's paid for by asking 33 seniors each to pay $6,000 more in health costs. That's not right. And it's not going to happen as long as I'm President. (Applause.)

This vision is less about reducing the deficit than it is about changing the basic social compact in America. Ronald Reagan's own budget director said, there's nothing "serious" or "courageous" about this plan. There's nothing serious about a plan that claims to reduce the deficit by spending a trillion dollars on tax cuts for millionaires and billionaires. And I don't think there's anything courageous about asking for sacrifice from those who can least afford it and don't have any clout on Capitol Hill. That's not a vision of the America I know.

The America I know is generous and compassionate. It's a land of opportunity and optimism. Yes, we take responsibility for ourselves, but we also take responsibility for each other; for the country we want and the future that we share. We're a nation that built a railroad across a continent and brought light to communities shrouded in darkness. We sent a generation to college on the GI Bill and we saved millions of seniors from poverty with Social Security and Medicare. We have led the world in scientific research and technological breakthroughs that have transformed millions of lives. That's who we are. This is the America that I know. We don't have to choose between a future of spiraling debt and one where we forfeit our investment in our people and our country.

To meet our fiscal challenge, we will need to make reforms. We will all need to make sacrifices. But we do not have to sacrifice the America we believe in. And as long as I'm President, we won't.

So today, I'm proposing a more balanced approach to achieve $4 trillion in deficit reduction over 12 years. It's an approach that borrows from the recommendations of the bipartisan Fiscal Commission that I appointed last year, and it builds on the roughly $1 trillion in deficit reduction I already proposed in my 2012 budget. It's an approach that puts every kind of spending on the table -- but one that protects the middle class, our promise to seniors, and our investments in the future.

The first step in our approach is to keep annual domestic spending low by building on the savings that both parties agreed to last week. That step alone will save us about $750 billion over 12 years. We will make the tough cuts necessary to achieve these savings, including in programs that I care deeply about, but I will not sacrifice the core investments that we need to grow and create jobs. We will invest in medical research. We will invest in clean energy technology. We will invest in new roads and airports and broadband access. We will invest in education. We will invest in job training. We will do what we need to do to compete, and we will win the future.

The second step in our approach is to find additional savings in our defense budget. Now, as Commander-in-Chief, I have no greater responsibility than protecting our national security, and I will never accept cuts that compromise our ability to defend our homeland or America's interests around the world. But as the Chairman of the Joint Chiefs, Admiral Mullen, has said, the greatest long-term threat to America's national security is America's debt. So just as we must find more savings in domestic programs, we must do the same in defense. And we can do that while still keeping ourselves safe.

Over the last two years, Secretary Bob Gates has courageously taken on wasteful spending, saving $400 billion in current and future spending. I believe we can do that again. We need to not only eliminate waste and improve efficiency and effectiveness, but we're going to have to conduct a fundamental review of America's missions, capabilities, and our role in a changing world. I intend to work with Secretary Gates and the Joint Chiefs on this review, and I will make specific decisions about spending after it's complete.

The third step in our approach is to further reduce health care spending in our budget. Now, here, the difference with the House Republican plan could not be clearer. Their plan essentially lowers the government's health care bills by asking seniors and poor families to pay them instead. Our approach lowers the government's health care bills by reducing the cost of health care itself.

Already, the reforms we passed in the health care law will reduce our deficit by $1 trillion. My approach would build on these reforms. We will reduce wasteful subsidies and erroneous payments. We will cut spending on prescription drugs by using Medicare's purchasing power to drive greater efficiency and speed generic brands of medicine onto the market. We will work with governors of both parties to demand more efficiency and accountability from Medicaid.

We will change the way we pay for health care -- not by the procedure or the number of days spent in a hospital, but with new

128

incentives for doctors and hospitals to prevent injuries and improve results. And we will slow the growth of Medicare costs by strengthening an independent commission of doctors, nurses, medical experts and consumers who will look at all the evidence and recommend the best ways to reduce unnecessary spending while protecting access to the services that seniors need.

Now, we believe the reforms we've proposed to strengthen Medicare and Medicaid will enable us to keep these commitments to our citizens while saving us $500 billion by 2023, and an additional $1 trillion in the decade after that. But if we're wrong, and Medicare costs rise faster than we expect, then this approach will give the independent commission the authority to make additional savings by further improving Medicare.

But let me be absolutely clear: I will preserve these health care programs as a promise we make to each other in this society. I will not allow Medicare to become a voucher program that leaves seniors at the mercy of the insurance industry, with a shrinking benefit to pay for rising costs. I will not tell families with children who have disabilities that they have to fend for themselves. We will reform these programs, but we will not abandon the fundamental commitment this country has kept for generations.

That includes, by the way, our commitment to Social Security. While Social Security is not the cause of our deficit, it faces real long-term challenges in a country that's growing older. As I said in the State of the Union, both parties should work together now to strengthen Social Security for future generations. But we have to do it without putting at risk current retirees, or the most vulnerable, or people with disabilities; without slashing benefits for future generations; and without subjecting Americans' guaranteed retirement income to the whims of the stock market. And it can be done.

The fourth step in our approach is to reduce spending in the tax code, so-called tax expenditures. In December, I agreed to extend the tax cuts for the wealthiest Americans because it was the only way I could prevent a tax hike on middle-class Americans. But we cannot afford $1 trillion worth of tax cuts for every millionaire and billionaire in our society. We can't afford it. And I refuse to renew them again.

Beyond that, the tax code is also loaded up with spending on things like itemized deductions. And while I agree with the goals of many of these deductions, from homeownership to charitable giving, we can't ignore the fact that they provide millionaires an average tax break of $75,000 but do nothing for the typical middle-class family that doesn't itemize. So my budget calls for limiting itemized deductions for the wealthiest 2 percent of Americans -- a reform that would reduce the deficit by $320 billion over 10 years.

But to reduce the deficit, I believe we should go further. And that's why I'm calling on Congress to reform our individual tax code so that it is fair and simple -- so that the amount of taxes you pay isn't determined by what kind of accountant you can afford.

I believe reform should protect the middle class, promote economic growth, and build on the fiscal commission's model of reducing tax expenditures so that there's enough savings to both lower rates and lower the deficit. And as I called for in the State of the Union, we should reform our corporate tax code as well, to make our businesses and our economy more competitive.

So this is my approach to reduce the deficit by $4 trillion over the next 12 years. It's an approach that achieves about $2 trillion in spending cuts across the budget. It will lower our interest payments on the debt by $1 trillion. It calls for tax reform to cut about $1 trillion in tax expenditures -- spending in the tax code. And it achieves these goals while protecting the middle class, protecting our commitment to seniors, and protecting our investments in the future.

Now, in the coming years, if the recovery speeds up and our economy grows faster than our current projections, we can make even greater progress than I've pledged here. But just to hold Washington -- and to hold me --- accountable and make sure that the debt burden continues to decline, my plan includes a debt failsafe. If, by 2014, our debt is not projected to fall as a share of the economy -– if we haven't hit our targets, if Congress has failed to act -- then my plan will require us to come together and make up the additional savings with more spending cuts and more spending reductions in the tax code. That should be an incentive for us to act boldly now, instead of kicking our problems further down the road.

So this is our vision for America -– this is my vision for America -- a vision where we live within our means while still investing in our future; where everyone makes sacrifices but no one bears all the burden; where we provide a basic measure of security for our citizens and we provide rising opportunity for our children.

There will be those who vigorously disagree with my approach. I can guarantee that as well. (Laughter.) Some will argue we should not even consider ever -- ever -- raising taxes, even if only on the wealthiest Americans. It's just an article of faith to them. I say that at a time when the tax burden on the wealthy is at its lowest level in half a century, the most fortunate among us can afford to pay a little more. I don't need another tax cut. Warren Buffett doesn't need another tax cut. Not if we have to pay for it by making seniors pay more for Medicare. Or by cutting kids from Head Start. Or by taking away college scholarships that I wouldn't be here without and that some of you would not be here without.

And here's the thing: I believe that most wealthy Americans would agree with me. They want to give back to their country, a country that's done so much for them. It's just Washington hasn't asked them to.

Others will say that we shouldn't even talk about cutting spending until the economy is fully recovered. These are mostly folks in my party. I'm sympathetic to this view -- which is one of the reasons I supported the payroll tax cuts we passed in December. It's also why we have to use a scalpel and not a machete to reduce the deficit, so that we can keep making the investments that create jobs. But doing nothing on the deficit is just not an option. Our debt has grown so large that we could do real damage to the economy if we don't begin a process now to get our fiscal house in order.

Finally, there are those who believe we shouldn't make any reforms to Medicare, Medicaid, or Social Security, out of fear that any talk of change to these programs will immediately usher in the sort of steps that the House Republicans have proposed. And I understand those fears. But I guarantee that if we don't make any changes at all, we won't be able to keep our commitment to a retiring generation that will live longer and will face higher health care costs than those who came before.

Indeed, to those in my own party, I say that if we truly believe in a progressive vision of our society, we have an obligation to prove that we can afford our commitments. If we believe the government can make a difference in people's lives, we have the obligation to prove that it works — by making government smarter, and leaner and more effective.

Of course, there are those who simply say there's no way we can come together at all and agree on a solution to this challenge. They'll say the politics of this city are just too broken; the choices are just too hard; the parties are just too far apart. And after a few years on this job, I have some sympathy for this view. (Laughter.)

But I also know that we've come together before and met big challenges. Ronald Reagan and Tip O'Neill came together to save Social Security for future generations. The first President Bush and a Democratic Congress came together to reduce the deficit. President Clinton and a Republican Congress battled each other ferociously, disagreed on just about everything, but they still found a way to balance the budget. And in the last few months, both parties have come together to pass historic tax relief and spending cuts.

And I know there are Republicans and Democrats in Congress who want to see a balanced approach to deficit reduction. And even those Republicans I disagree with most strongly I believe are sincere about wanting to do right by their country. We may disagree on our visions, but I truly believe they want to do the right thing.

So I believe we can, and must, come together again. This morning, I met with Democratic and Republican leaders in Congress to discuss the approach that I laid out today. And in early May, the Vice President will begin regular meetings with leaders in both parties with the aim of reaching a final agreement on a plan to reduce the deficit and get it done by the end of June.

I don't expect the details in any final agreement to look exactly like the approach I laid out today. This a democracy; that's not how things work. I'm eager to hear other ideas from all ends of the political spectrum. And though I'm sure the criticism of what I've said here today will be fierce in some quarters, and my critique of the House Republican approach has been strong, Americans deserve and will demand that we all make an effort to bridge our differences and find common ground.

This larger debate that we're having -- this larger debate about the size and the role of government -- it has been with us since our founding days. And during moments of great challenge and change, like the one that we're living through now, the debate gets sharper and it gets more vigorous. That's not a bad thing. In fact, it's a good thing. As a country that prizes both our individual freedom and our obligations to one another, this is one of the most important debates that we can have.

But no matter what we argue, no matter where we stand, we've always held certain beliefs as Americans. We believe that in order to preserve our own freedoms and pursue our own happiness, we can't just think about ourselves. We have to think about the country that made these liberties possible. We have to think about our fellow citizens with whom we share a community. And we have to think about what's required to preserve the American Dream for future generations.

This sense of responsibility -- to each other and to our country -- this isn't a partisan feeling. It isn't a Democratic or a Republican idea. It's patriotism.

The other day I received a letter from a man in Florida. He started off by telling me he didn't vote for me and he hasn't always agreed with me. But even though he's worried about our economy and the state of our politics -- here's what he said -- he said, "I still believe. I believe in that great country that my grandfather told me about. I believe that somewhere lost in this quagmire of petty bickering on every news station, the 'American Dream' is still alive...We need to use our dollars here rebuilding, refurbishing and restoring all that our ancestors struggled to create and maintain... We as a people must do this together, no matter the color of the state one comes from or the side of the aisle one might sit on."

"I still believe." I still believe as well. And I know that if we can come together and uphold our responsibilities to one another and to this larger enterprise that is America, we will keep the dream of our founding alive -- in our time; and we will pass it on to our children. We will pass on to our children a country that we believe in.

Thank you. God bless you, and may God bless the United States of

America. (Applause.)
END
2:31 P.M. EDT

APPENDIX B: ALGORITHM FOR CALCULATING POLITICAL POWER

Political Party Affiliation for the US Senate (Sscore). To measure the relative strength of the Sscore, the strength of party dominance (positive for the Republican Party [RP] and negative for the Democratic Party [DP]) is calculated by the relative difference in seats occupied.

- For each year,
  - Let Democrat Senators (DS) = the number of DP senators
  - Let Republican Senators (RS) = the number of RP senators
  - Let total senators (TS) = the total number of senators
- Then, for each year,

$$\text{Sscore} = ((-1)(DS/TS) + (RS/TS))*100$$

Political Party Affiliation for the House of Representatives (Hscore). To measure the relative strength of the Hscore, the strength of party dominance (positive for RP and negative for DP) is calculated by the relative difference in seats occupied.

- For each year,
  - Let Democrat Representatives (DH) = the number of DP representatives
  - Let Republican Representatives (RH) = the number of RP representatives
  - Let TH = the total number of representatives
- Then, for each year,

$$\text{Hscore} = ((-1)(DH/TH) + (RH/TH))*100$$

Political Party Affiliation of the Congress (Cscore). Cscore is the combined Sscore and Hscore for each year.

Data for the analysis is from

- Sscore data are from
  http://www.senate.gov/pagelayout/history/one_item_and_

teasers/ partydiv.htm; and
http://www.senate.gov/artandhistory/history/resources/
pdf/chronlist.pdf.

* Hscore data are from
http://artandhistory.house.gov/house_history/partyDiv.aspx.

Data are summarized in the following figure.

Session	Senate					House					President	
	Dem	Rep	Other	Vacant	Total	Dem	Rep	Other	Vacant	Total	Dem	Rep
1933-1934	59	36	1	0	96	313	117	5	0	435	F. Roosevelt	
1935-1936	69	25	2	0	96	332	103	10	0	445	F. Roosevelt	
1937-1938	76	16	4	0	96	334	88	13	0	435	F. Roosevelt	
1939-1940	69	23	4	0	96	262	169	4	0	435	F. Roosevelt	
1941-1942	66	28	2	0	96	276	162	6	0	444	F. Roosevelt	
1943-1944	57	38	1	0	96	222	209	4	0	435	F. Roosevelt	
1945-1946	57	38	1	0	96	242	191	2	0	435	Truman	
1947-1948	45	51	0	0	96	188	246	1	0	435	Truman	
1949-1950	54	42	0	0	96	263	171	1	0	435	Truman	
1951-1952	49	47	0	0	96	235	199	1	0	435	Truman	
1953-1954	47	48	1	0	96	213	221	1	0	435		Eisenhower
1955-1956	48	47	1	0	96	232	203	0	0	435		Eisenhower
1957-1958	49	47	0	0	96	234	201	0	0	435		Eisenhower
1959-1960	65	35	0	0	100	283	153	1	0	437		Eisenhower
1961-1962	64	36	0	0	100	263	174	0	0	437	Kennedy	
1963-1964	66	34	0	0	100	259	176	0	0	435	Johnson	
1965-1966	68	32	0	0	100	295	140	0	0	435	Johnson	
1967-1968	64	36	0	0	100	247	187	0	1	435	Johnson	
1969-1970	57	43	0	0	100	243	192	0	0	435		Nixon
1971-1972	54	44	2	0	100	255	180	0	0	435		Nixon
1973-1974	56	42	2	0	100	242	192	1	0	435		Nixon/Ford
1975-1976	60	38	2	0	100	291	144	0	0	435		Ford
1977-1978	61	38	1	0	100	292	143	0	0	435	Carter	
1979-1980	58	41	1	0	100	277	158	0	0	435	Carter	
1981-1982	46	53	1	0	100	242	192	1	0	435		Reagan
1983-1984	46	54	0	0	100	269	166	0	0	435		Reagan
1985-1986	47	53	0	0	100	253	182	0	0	435		Reagan
1987-1988	55	45	0	0	100	258	177	0	0	435		Reagan
1989-1990	55	45	0	0	100	260	175	0	0	435		G. H. W. Bush
1991-1992	56	44	0	0	100	267	167	1	0	435		G. H. W. Bush
1993-1994	56	44	0	0	100	258	176	1	0	435	Clinton	
1995-1996	47	53	0	0	100	204	230	1	0	435	Clinton	
1997-1998	45	55	0	0	100	206	228	1	0	435	Clinton	
1999-2000	45	55	0	0	100	211	223	1	0	435	Clinton	
2001-2002	48	50	2	0	100	212	221	1	0	434		G. W. Bush
2003-2004	48	51	1	0	100	204	229	1	1	435		G. W. Bush
2005-2006	44	55	1	0	100	202	232	1	0	435		G. W. Bush
2007-2008	49	49	2	0	100	233	202	0	0	435		G.W. Bush
2009-2010	58	40	2	0	100	257	178	0	0	435	Obama	
2011-2012	51	47	2	0	100	193	242	0	0	435	Obama	

Figure 14. Data on Political Party Composition of the Senate, House, and Presidency between 1933 and 2012

APPENDIX C: TRANSCRIPT OF REMARKS BY PRESIDENT OBAMA ON HEALTH INSURANCE REFORM

The White House[216]
Office of the Press Secretary
For Immediate Release
March 22, 2010
East Room
11:47 P.M. EDT
THE PRESIDENT: Good evening, everybody. Tonight, after nearly 100 years of talk and frustration, after decades of trying, and a year of sustained effort and debate, the United States Congress finally declared that America's workers and America's families and America's small businesses deserve the security of knowing that here, in this country, neither illness nor accident should endanger the dreams they've worked a lifetime to achieve.

Tonight, at a time when the pundits said it was no longer possible, we rose above the weight of our politics. We pushed back on the undue influence of special interests. We didn't give in to mistrust or to cynicism or to fear. Instead, we proved that we are still a people capable of doing big things and tackling our biggest challenges. We proved that this government -- a government of the people and by the people -- still works for the people.

I want to thank every member of Congress who stood up tonight with courage and conviction to make health care reform a reality. And I

---

[216] The Remarks by the President were retrieved from
http://www.whitehouse.gov/the-press-office/remarks-president-house-vote-health-insurance-reform

know this wasn't an easy vote for a lot of people. But it was the right vote. I want to thank Speaker Nancy Pelosi for her extraordinary leadership, and Majority Leader Steny Hoyer and Majority Whip Jim Clyburn for their commitment to getting the job done. I want to thank my outstanding Vice President, Joe Biden, and my wonderful Secretary of Health and Human Services, Kathleen Sebelius, for their fantastic work on this issue. I want to thank the many staffers in Congress, and my own incredible staff in the White House, who have worked tirelessly over the past year with Americans of all walks of life to forge a reform package finally worthy of the people we were sent here to serve.

Today's vote answers the dreams of so many who have fought for this reform. To every unsung American who took the time to sit down and write a letter or type out an e-mail hoping your voice would be heard -- it has been heard tonight. To the untold numbers who knocked on doors and made phone calls, who organized and mobilized out of a firm conviction that change in this country comes not from the top down, but from the bottom up -- let me reaffirm that conviction: This moment is possible because of you.

Most importantly, today's vote answers the prayers of every American who has hoped deeply for something to be done about a health care system that works for insurance companies, but not for ordinary people. For most Americans, this debate has never been about abstractions, the fight between right and left, Republican and Democrat -- it's always been about something far more personal. It's about every American who knows the shock of opening an envelope to see that their premiums just shot up again when times are already tough enough. It's about every parent who knows the desperation of trying to cover a child with a chronic illness only to be told "no" again and again and again. It's about every small business owner forced to choose between insuring employees and staying open for business. They are why we committed ourselves to this cause.

Tonight's vote is not a victory for any one party -- it's a victory for them. It's a victory for the American people. And it's a victory for common sense.

Now, it probably goes without saying that tonight's vote will give rise to a frenzy of instant analysis. There will be tallies of Washington winners and losers, predictions about what it means for Democrats and Republicans, for my poll numbers, for my administration. But long after the debate fades away and the prognostication fades away and the dust settles, what will remain standing is not the government-run system some feared, or the status quo that serves the interests of the insurance industry, but a health care system that incorporates ideas from both parties -- a system that works better for the American people.

If you have health insurance, this reform just gave you more control by reining in the worst excesses and abuses of the insurance industry with some of the toughest consumer protections this country has ever known -- so that you are actually getting what you pay for.

If you don't have insurance, this reform gives you a chance to be a part of a big purchasing pool that will give you choice and competition and cheaper prices for insurance. And it includes the largest health care tax cut for working families and small businesses in history -- so that if you lose your job and you change jobs, start that new business, you'll finally be able to purchase quality, affordable care and the security and peace of mind that comes with it.

This reform is the right thing to do for our seniors. It makes Medicare stronger and more solvent, extending its life by almost a decade. And it's the right thing to do for our future. It will reduce our deficit by more than $100 billion over the next decade, and more than $1 trillion in the decade after that.

So this isn't radical reform. But it is major reform. This legislation will not fix everything that ails our health care system. But it moves us decisively in the right direction. This is what change looks like.

Now as momentous as this day is, it's not the end of this journey. On Tuesday, the Senate will take up revisions to this legislation that the House has embraced, and these are revisions that have strengthened this law and removed provisions that had no place in it. Some have predicted another siege of parliamentary maneuvering in order to delay adoption of these improvements. I hope that's not the case. It's time to bring this debate to a close and begin the hard work of implementing this reform properly on behalf of the American people. This year, and in years to come, we have a solemn responsibility to do it right.

Nor does this day represent the end of the work that faces our country. The work of revitalizing our economy goes on. The work of promoting private sector job creation goes on. The work of putting American families' dreams back within reach goes on. And we march on, with renewed confidence, energized by this victory on their behalf.

In the end, what this day represents is another stone firmly laid in the foundation of the American Dream. Tonight, we answered the call of history as so many generations of Americans have before us. When faced with crisis, we did not shrink from our challenge -- we overcame it. We did not avoid our responsibility -- we embraced it. We did not fear our future -- we shaped it.

Thank you, God bless you, and may God bless the United States of America.
END
11:55 P.M. EDT

INDEX

ABOUT THE AUTHOR

**Ronald J. Scott, Jr., Ph.D.**, is founder and principal consultant at Vectored Solutions, LLC. He served over 30 years in the U.S. Air Force, as a command and instructor pilot in fighter and airlift aircraft, commanding units on global assignments and directing the Air Force's global operations center at the Pentagon. He more recently consulted for a Washington-area applied research firm providing strategic analysis related to counterterrorism. He currently serves as an adjunct professor, teaching ethics and research methodology, and mentoring doctoral candidates through the dissertation process. His theoretical and analytical work has been published in academic peer-reviewed journals.

www.ingramcontent.com/pod-product-compliance
Lightning Source LLC
Chambersburg PA
CBHW071044290526
45795CB00004B/1316